Terrors of the Deep

By Deborah Lock

LONDON, NEW YORK, MUNICH, MELBOURNE, AND DELHI

DK LONDON
Series Editor Deborah Lock
Project Editor Camilla Gersh
US Senior Editor Shannon Betty
Production Editor Francesca Wardell
Illustrator Eoin Coveney
Reading Consultant Linda Gambrell, Ph.D.

DK DELHI
Editor Nandini Gupta
Assistant Art Editor Yamini Panwar
DTP Designer Anita Yadav
Picture Researcher Sakshi Saluja
Deputy Managing Editor Soma B. Chowdhury
Design Consultant Shefali Upadhyay

First American Edition, 2014
Published in the United States by
DK Publishing, 345 Hudson Street, New York, New York 10014
14 15 16 17 18 10 9 8 7 6 5 4 3 2
001—195865—January/2014

Published in Great Britain by Dorling Kindersley Limited.
A catalog record for this book is available from the Library of Congress.
ISBN: 978-1-4654-1722-0 (pb)
ISBN: 978-1-4654-1812-8 (plc)

Printed and bound by C&C Offset Printing Co. Ltd..
The publisher would like to thank Lieutenant James Binns RN for his advice.
The publisher would like to thank the following for their kind permission to reproduce their photographs:
(Key: a-above; b-below/bottom; c-centre; f-far; l-left; r-right; t-top)
1 Corbis: Wim van Egmond / Visuals Unlimited (c). **3 Corbis**: Ocean. **8 Fotolia**: spaxiax (tr). **16-17 Corbis**: Scubazoo / SuperStock (b). **19 Alamy Images**: National Geographic Image Collection (t). **21 Alamy Images**: WoodyStock. **22 Dorling Kindersley**: Courtesy of MarineLand (cla). **23 Corbis**: (tr). **25 Dorling Kindersley**: Courtesy of the Weymouth Sea Life Centre (clb); Laszlo Veres (tl). **Science Photo Library**: Win Van Egmond / Visuals Unlimited, Inc. (bl). **29 Corbis**: Lynda Richardson (b). **Dreamstime.com**: Luis Viegas (b/Frame). **30 Dreamstime.com**: Luis Viegas (t/Frame). **NOAA**: (tl). **33 Alamy Images**: Snaprender (b). **35 Dreamstime.com**: Luis Viegas (b/Frame). **Science Photo Library**: Dante Fenolio (b). **37 Alamy Images**: Epicscotland (bl). **40 NOAA**: (cl). Science Photo Library: Dante Fenolio (br); Alexander Semenov (tr). **41 Alamy Images**: Mark Conlin (tl). **Getty Images**: De Agostini Picture Library (bl). **Science Photo Library**: Dante Fenolio (cr). **46-47 Dreamstime.com**: Mexrix (t). **48 Alamy Images**: Brandon Cole Marine Photography (br). **Dreamstime.com**: Luis Viegas (br/Frame). **51 Alamy Images**: AF archive (b). **55 Corbis**: Jacob Maentz (tr). **58 Corbis**: Gerald & Buff Corsi / Visuals Unlimited (cra). **NOAA**: Pacific Ring of Fire 2004 Expedition. NOAA Office of Ocean Exploration; Dr. Bob Embley, NOAA PMEL, Chief Scientist (cl, crb). **58-59 NOAA**: OAR / National Undersea Research Program (NURP) (c). **59 NOAA**: NOAA Submarine Ring of Fire 2004 (Volcanoes Unit MTMNM) (crb); Pacific Ring of Fire 2004 Expedition. NOAA Office of Ocean Exploration; Dr. Bob Embley, NOAA PMEL, Chief Scientist (tc); SEFSC Pascagoula Laboratory; Collection of Brandi Noble (ca). **63 Dreamstime.com**: Zoran Matic. **64 Alamy Images**: Amanda Cotton. **68-69 Alamy Images**: Amanda Cotton (b). **71 Dreamstime.com**: Dmytro Denysov (t). **72 Dreamstime.com**: Makhnach (t). **74 Mary Evans Picture Library**: (tr, bl). **75 Getty Images**: Handout (tr). **80-81 Dreamstime.com**: Photoeuphoria (b). **82 Dreamstime.com**: Luis Viegas (t/Frame). **NOAA**: IFE, URI-IAO, UW, Lost City Science Party (t). **85 Dreamstime.com**: Luis Viegas (b/Frame). **NOAA**: Monterey Bay Aquarium Research Institute (b). **87 Corbis**: Jeffrey Rotman. **90 NOAA**: Charleston Bump Expedition 2003. NOAA Office of Ocean Exploration; Dr. George Sedberry, South Carolina DNR, Principal Investigator (bl); IFE, URI-IAO, UW, Lost City Science Party (cra). **90-91 Corbis**: Ralph A. Clevenger (b). **91 NOAA**: Monterey Bay Aquarium Research Institute (tr, br); SEFSC Pascagoula Laboratory; Collection of Brandi Noble, NOAA / NMFS / SEFSC (cla); Hidden Ocean 2005 Expedition: NOAA Office of Ocean Exploration (clb). **92 Alamy Images**: Randy Duchaine (cl). **Science Photo Library**: Stan Wayman (br). **93 Corbis**: Ralph White (bl); Zhang Xudong / Xinhua Press (ca). **99 Corbis**: Flip Nicklin / Minden Pictures (t). **100 Corbis**: Norbert Wu / Minden Pictures (t). **105 Dorling Kindersley**: Courtesy of the Natural History Museum, London (ca, tl). **108 Alamy Images**: National Geographic Image Collection (crb). **108-109 Dorling Kindersley**: Courtesy of the Natural History Museum, London. **109 Dorling Kindersley**: Courtesy of the Natural History Museum, London (bl). **111 Corbis**: David Fleetham / Visuals Unlimited. **122 Alamy Images**: AF archive (crb). **123 Dorling Kindersley**: Courtesy of the Natural History Museum, London (b). **124 Dreamstime.com**: Cornelius20 (tr). **125 Pearson Asset Library**: Cheuk-king Lo (cr)
Jacket images: Front: Ocean / **Corbis**; **Back** (r) Amanda Cotton / **Alamy**
Spine: Jeff Hornbaker / Water Rights / **Corbis**

All other images © Dorling Kindersley
For further information see: www.dkimages.com

Discover more at
www.dk.com

Contents

The Location

Under the ocean, there are deep valleys called trenches. The trenches are the deepest places on Earth, and the deepest of them all is the Mariana Trench in the Pacific Ocean.

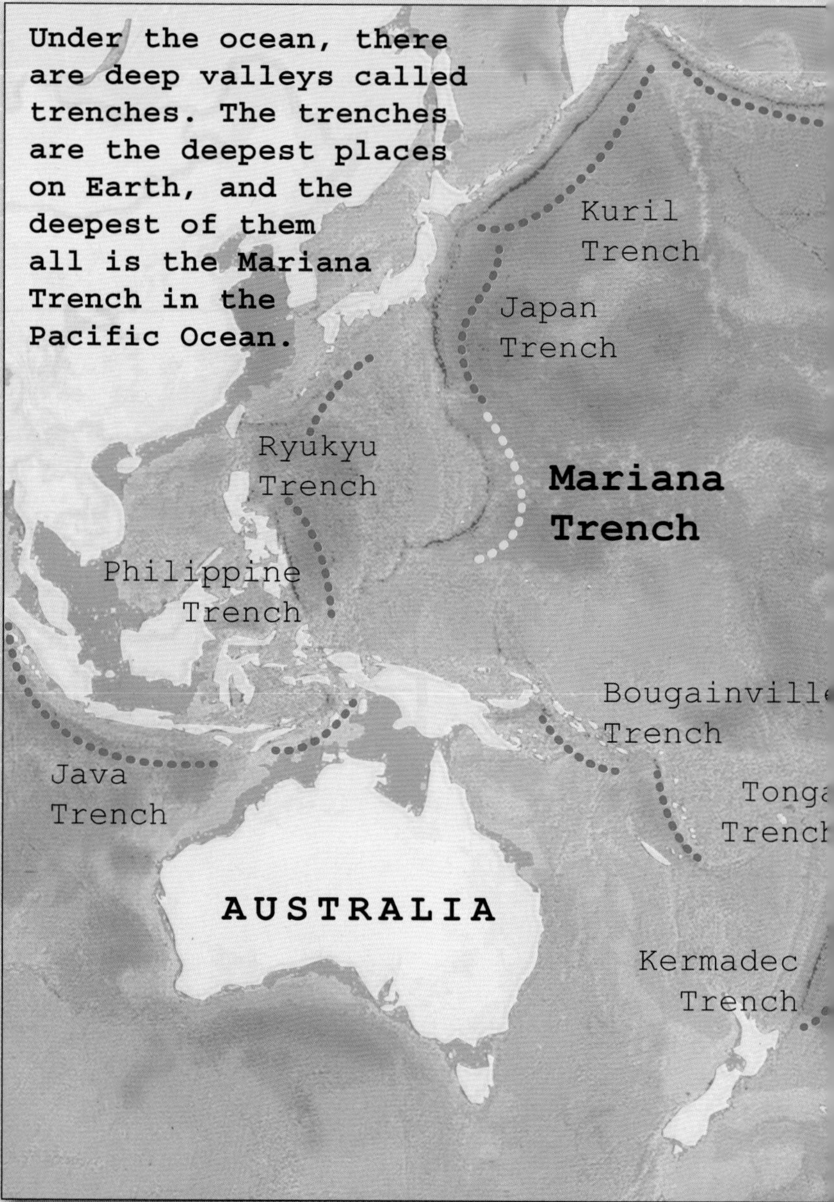

Kuril Trench

Japan Trench

Ryukyu Trench

Mariana Trench

Philippine Trench

Bougainville Trench

Java Trench

Tonga Trench

AUSTRALIA

Kermadec Trench

Aleutian Trench

NORTH AMERICA

NORTH PACIFIC OCEAN

Middle American Trench

SOUTH PACIFIC OCEAN

Peru-Chile Trench

Meet the Team

Our team of explorers is setting off on a mission to explore the deepest part of the ocean. Two people will dive down in the submersible *Orion*. They will be monitored on the surface by a crew on the support ship *Andromeda*.

ANDROMEDA SUPPORT SHIP

KARL FISCHER
Captain

JESS SALMON
Navigator

NICK ZANDER
Transmitter operator

RAOUL MOULE
Support swimmer for launch and retrieval

BEN PIKE
Crane operator for launch and retrieval

ORION SUBMERSIBLE

DOM MARLIN
Marine biologist, navigator

JAKE STURGEON
Pilot

Prologue

The digits on the Global Positioning System (GPS) read 11°21'N 142°12'E.

"We're right above the Mariana Trench, Karl," said Jess, glancing up from the navigational screen.

"Great! Let Dom and Jake know," instructed Karl, the captain, as he stopped the engines of *Andromeda*. "We'll launch the sub in three hours."

Jess found Dom and Jake on the upper deck. Dom was looking out at the sunrise on the horizon. The golden glow reflected on the calm ocean.

"These are perfect conditions for the launch," said Dom.

"It'll be the last time we'll see the sunlight for a while," replied Jake.

"Yes, no light reaches where we're going," said Dom. He checked his watch.

"It's time to do a final check over *Orion*. Did you fill up the hydraulic fluid for the robotic arm?"

"Yes," replied Jake. "I wonder what specimens we'll pick up and bring back to the surface."

"We're likely to find new species," remarked Dom. "Perhaps they'll be named after you or me?"

Jake and Dom laughed as they headed down the steps to the lower deck, where the submersible *Orion* was sitting in her launch cradle.

"Isn't she a beauty?" Dom said proudly, stroking the metallic hull of the gleaming sub. "I have no doubt she'll take care of us over the next 24 hours."

"Designed to perfection—we'd better take good care of her, too!" exclaimed Jake. "Anyway, I'm going to get into my gear. See you back here at 11:00 for pre-launch checks."

Pre-launch Checks

CHECK 1
Power up thrusters. Twist thrusters forward, backward, up, and down for maneuvering.

CHECK 2
Turn tail fins to left and right for steering.

CHECK 3
Switch on and off LED search lights and lasers.

CHECK 4
Check oxygen supply levels are enough for 24-hour mission.

CHECK 5
Check hydraulic fluid levels are full and check the suction sampler and robotic manipulator are working.

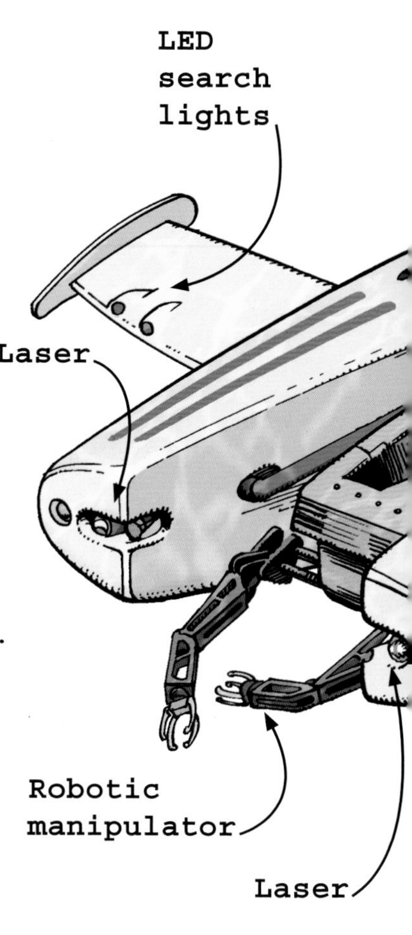

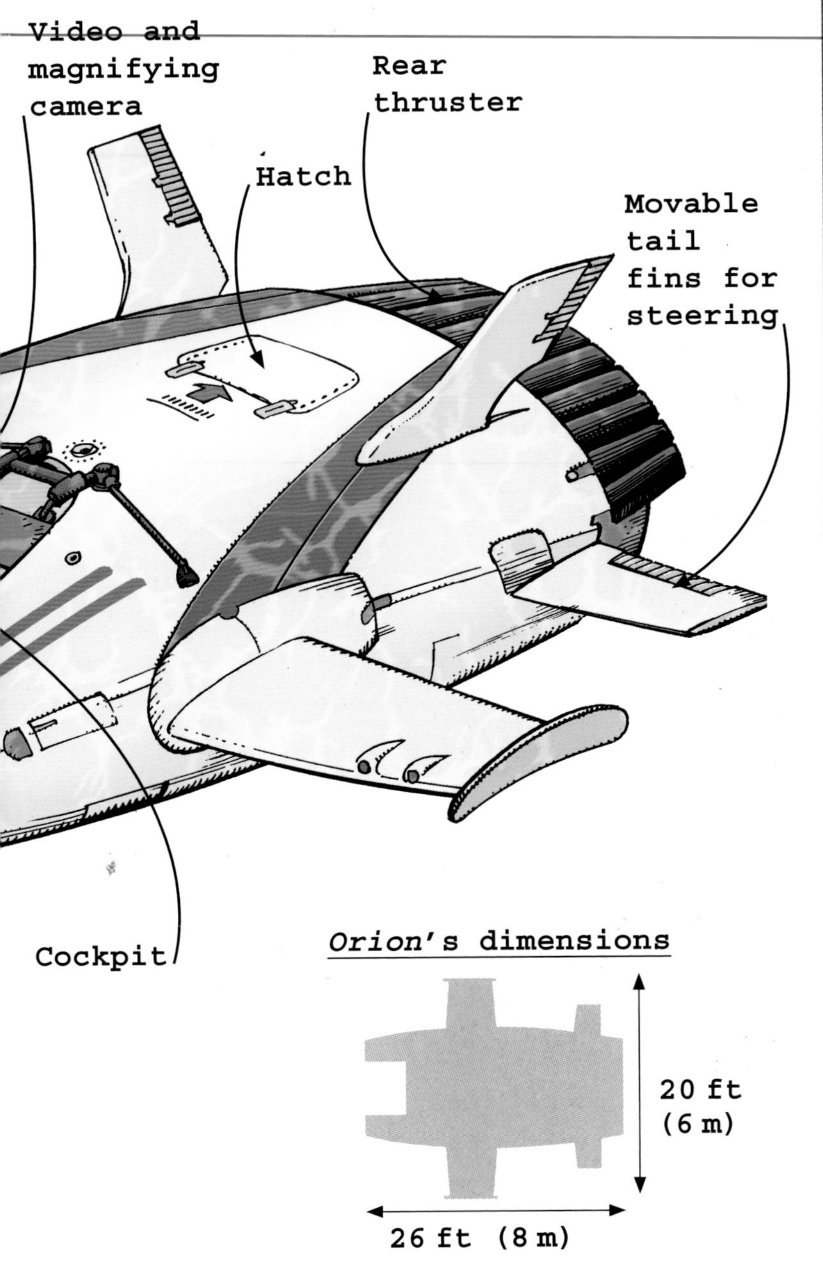
Video and magnifying camera
Rear thruster
Hatch
Movable tail fins for steering
Cockpit
Orion's dimensions
20 ft (6 m)
26 ft (8 m)

Chapter 1 The Launch

Dom turned to wave at the crew of *Andromeda* just before slipping through the hatch. He wriggled through to the cockpit, where Jake had already positioned himself in the pilot's seat.

"Sitting comfortably?" asked Dom.

"Not too bad," replied Jake. "At least there's leg room."

"Yes, that was one of my requirements when designing this beauty."

"How are the pre-launch checks going?" crackled Nick's voice over the transmitter. Nick was the operator and would be their contact with *Andromeda* until halfway down.

"All seems to be working perfectly," responded Jake. "Did you see how smoothly those hydraulic thrusters swiveled? That'll mean magnificent maneuverability."

Dom strapped himself into his seat and then gave the thumbs up out of the viewing window. "We're good to go," he said into the transmitter.

On top of *Orion*, Raoul, the support swimmer had sealed the hatch and was leaning against the crane's sturdy lift cables. Ben at the crane's controls signaled to him, and Raoul stood up ready for the launch. The crane's cables creaked as they took the strain of *Orion*'s tremendous weight. Then, slowly, Ben at the controls gently swung *Orion* out over the ocean and lowered her into the water.

Within seconds, the water was lapping over the top hatch. Raoul attached a towrope from the small support boat already in the water and unhooked the crane's cables. The boat towed *Orion* a short distance away from *Andromeda*.

Inside *Orion*, Jake turned on the hydraulic thrusters, ready to take over control to dive. 200 feet from the ship, Raoul unclipped the towrope, dived into the water, and swam to the support boat.

Orion was on her own.

"That took 5 minutes 28 seconds—a perfect launch," said Nick. "It looked great from here. How was it for you guys?"

"The swing out was a rocky ride but everything is wonderfully smooth now as we glide through the water," replied Dom.

"We're not the only ones gliding. Look over there," said Jake, pointing ahead of them.

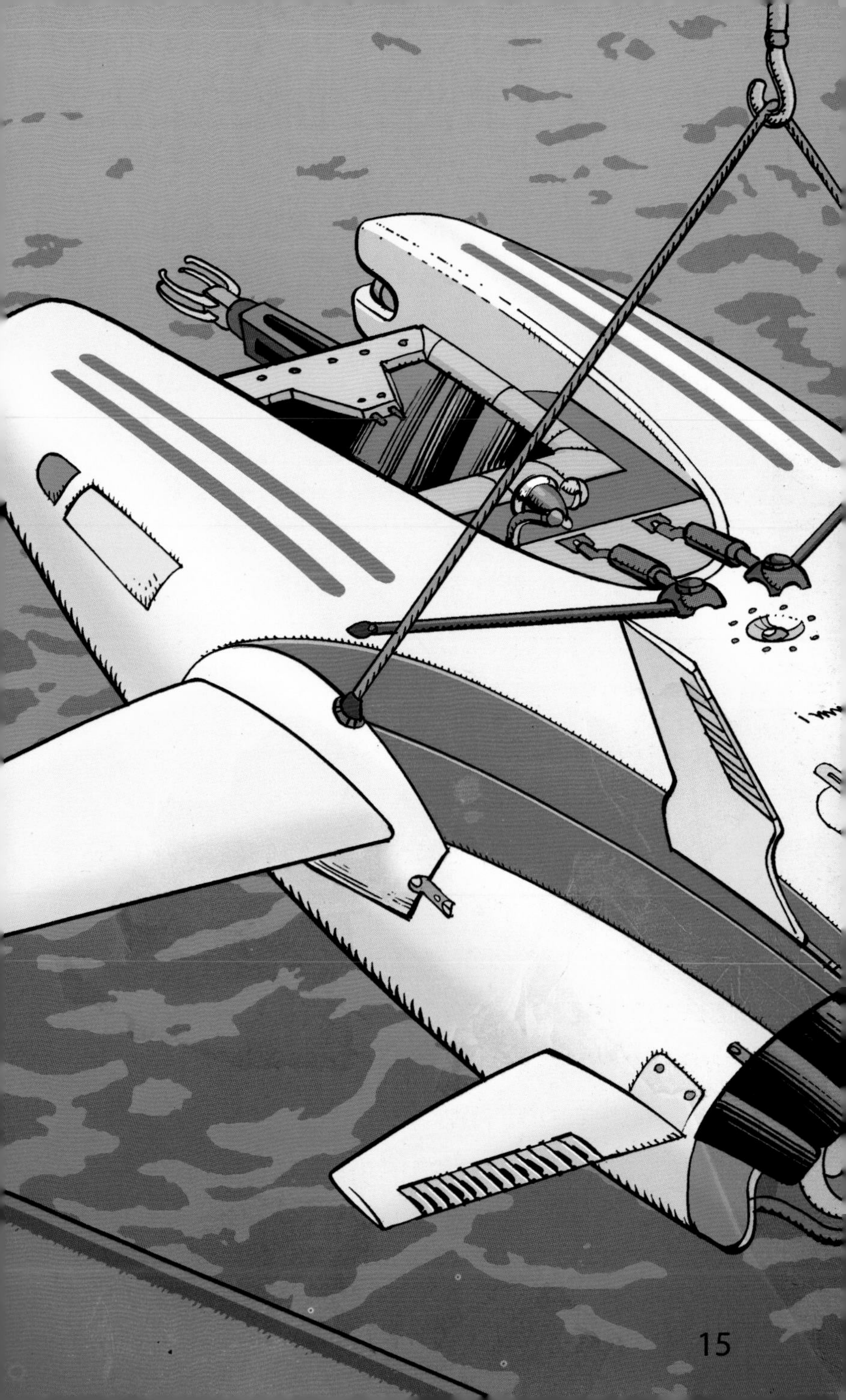

Ahead through the sunlit blue ocean, giant manta rays majestically waved their large, powerful, winglike fins up and down. From beneath, their white bellies glimmered in the sun's rays. Jake steered *Orion* closer to them.

Dom turned on the high-definition underwater video system. He zoomed the camera in close on one ray. Small

wrasse and a couple of two-foot-long remoras could be seen swimming alongside and then darting into the manta's body to nibble at parasites on its skin. Others were close to the manta's vast cavernous mouth, feeding on pieces of food, while some even bravely darted into the gill cavities—the part of the mouth where the plankton was sifted out of the water.

"Are you getting this clearly?" asked Dom through the transmitter to Nick up top.

"Yes, the camera is relaying well. How many mantas are there?"

"I've counted six," said Jake, leaning forward to get a view from a different angle through the window.

"I'll keep the camera on so you can see the action," transmitted Dom. "We have a shoal of mackerel cruising off to our starboard side. They don't seem frightened by us as we glide silently by. It's like we're flying through the water as we intended *Orion* to do."

"There are a couple of leatherback turtles just below us," spied Jake.

"They must be between nesting grounds in Indonesia and their feeding sites in the South China Sea," informed Dom.

"That first one is almost as big as a person."

"Yes, more than two and a half feet long—a pretty incredible size."

"Something's just scared the mackerel. Look—they're forming into a ball."

"It's bottlenose dolphins! A pod of them are circling the mackerel," said Dom. He switched on the hydrophone listening system. The cockpit was filled with the noise of dolphin clicks and squeaks.

"They're a chatty bunch," remarked Jake.

"They must be anticipating a feast for their lunch."

Jake turned the sub so they could both watch from a safe distance.

The water swirled as the dolphins flashed around the shoal. The mackerel moved into an ever-tighter ball, circling. Their silver scales glinted where the sunlight peeked through. Then suddenly, the dolphins changed tactics and flashed in and out of the ball, catching mackerel.

The scattered mackerel, panicked and confused, tried to re-form for safety. The dolphins turned with greater agility and picked them off gulps at a time. The attack was a ferocious frenzy. Then, as suddenly as it had begun, the action was all over. The dolphins, having eaten their fill, zipped off into the distance, with some leaping out of the water.

"We can see them leaping from here," transmitted Nick. "Awesome!"

"It's a great start," replied Dom, "but we'll never reach the bottom if we hang around here. Let's dive."

?
What adjectives would you use to describe this mackerel ball?

Dolphin Fact File

LENGTH: 6.5–13 ft (2–4 m)
WEIGHT: 331.5–442 lb (150–200 kg)
SPEED: up to 25 mph (40 kph)
PREDATORS: human and shark

BLOWHOLE works like a nose and is used for breathing. When a dolphin rises to the surface, it can shoot water from its blowhole at up to 100 mph (160 kph).

LARGE, COMPLEX BRAIN indicates high level of intelligence.

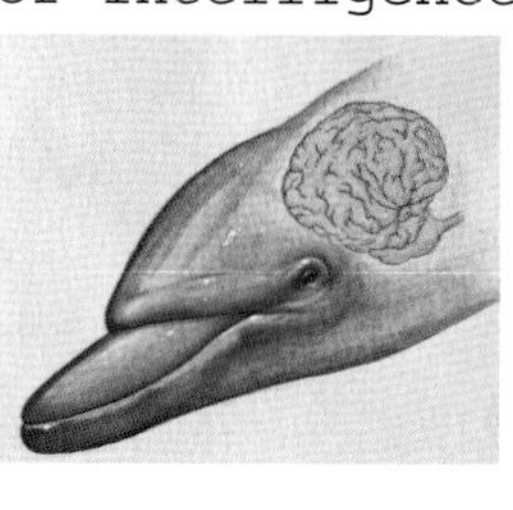

CONE-SHAPED TEETH are used to grip food, not to chew. Bottlenose dolphins have more than 100 teeth.

TWO STOMACHS: one for storing food and one for digesting it. Dolphins may eat about 30 lb (14 kg) of fish a day.

INTELLIGENCE: dolphins use tools such as shells, live in groups, and use teamwork to catch fish. They are capable of communication and can understand up to 60 words.

BLUBBER is a layer of fat underneath the skin. It gives the dolphin the ideal shape for fast swimming and helps to maintain body temperature.

TAIL FLIPPERS (flukes) are about 23 in. (60 cm) in width. They move up and down to propel the dolphin through water.

Sunlit Zone Marine Food Chains

Within the sunlit zone of the ocean, tiny living things called plankton are eaten by small sea creatures. These creatures are then eaten by larger sea creatures, which are eaten by still larger animals, and so on.

Great white shark

SHARKS are at the top of the food chain, with virtually no predators. Larger species, such as great white sharks, eat dolphins as well as fish and other sea animals.

Bottlenose dolphin

BOTTLENOSE DOLPHINS eat squid and all sorts of fish, including cod and herring.

Cod

COD and other larger fish eat smaller fish, such as herring.

Herring

HERRING and SPRATS live on small animals called plankton and are eaten by larger animals.

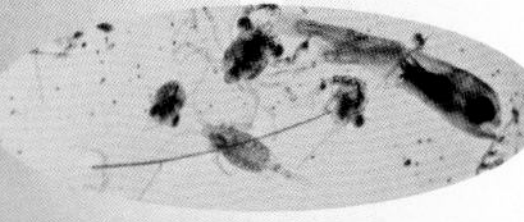

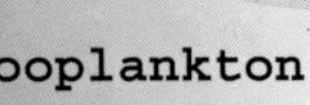

Zooplankton

ZOOPLANKTON are small animals, such as jellyfish or crustaceans, that eat only phytoplankton.

Phytoplankton

PHYTOPLANKTON are small, plantlike living things that use the light of the sun to make their own food, using a process called photosynthesis.

SEA LEVEL

1,000 fathoms

2,000 fathoms

3,000 fathoms

4,000 fathoms

5,000 fathoms

6,000 fathoms

Chapter 2
200 - 2,000 Fathoms Deep

"We're past the continental shelf and entering the trench," said Jake, levering the control stick. "The peaks of these underwater seamounts require some skill navigating around."

"This rim is the widest part. As we get deeper, your piloting skills will definitely be put to the test. Our plan is to travel along the trench for a bit," continued Dom, "to check out life around the hydrothermal volcanic vents and then descend into Challenger Deep."

"Shall I turn on the light-emitting diode (LED) lights? Otherwise we won't be able to see a thing down here in the complete darkness."

"Would you still be able to pilot around these rocks if we kept them dim? We may scare the creatures with the full lights on."

"OK. The lasers should provide enough guidance to probe what's coming up ahead for the time being. What do you expect to see?" asked Jake.

"Those lanternfish over there for a start," said Dom, pointing out of the port side.

In the dimmed lights from *Orion*, fish about 6 inches long, with glowing lights along their undersides, slowly drifted past.

Dom maneuvered the magnifying camera into position above the sub like a periscope and turned it on. The screen in front of him showed an ocean teeming with glimmering microorganisms.

"Do you recognize any?" asked Jake.

"Those wavy worms are green bombers," Dom said excitedly. "They release tiny glowing bombs when they sense danger and start swimming backward to distract and escape from predators. It looks as though that's what they're doing now to avoid us."

"Is that a water spider?" questioned Jake. He pointed to a bizarre, six-legged creature on the screen that looked like it was attempting to walk in the water to move.

"It's known as a *munnopsis isopod*, and scientists think millions of years ago this species probably learned to walk before it could swim. If you look closely, it's either swimming by striding forward or pedaling backward, or escaping rapidly, swimming backward like other crustaceans."

"It now looks like it's just hanging out at the moment."

"Yes, it does," chuckled Dom. "Its long legs are spread out to stop it from sinking."

SEA LEVEL
1,000 fathoms
2,000 fathoms
3,000 fathoms
4,000 fathoms
5,000 fathoms
6,000 fathoms

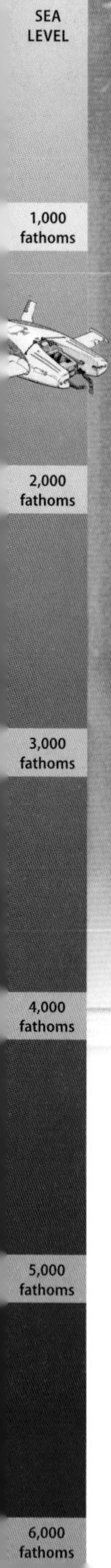

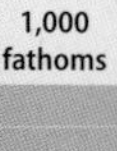

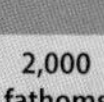

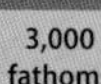

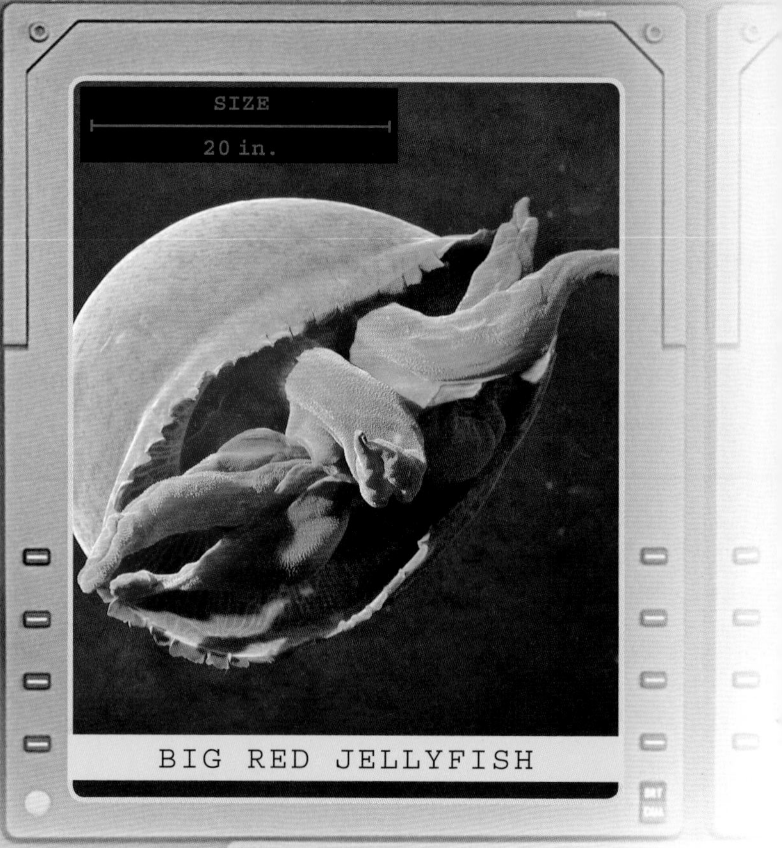

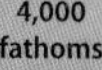

SIZE
20 in.
BIG RED JELLYFISH

“It looks like there is a big creature ahead of us,” said Jake.

“It’s a dumbo octopus,” responded Dom. Then as the sub moved closer, he said, “No! I’m mistaken—it’s a big red jellyfish.”

“You’re joking! That’s what the

marine experts have called it—a big red jellyfish?"

"That's what it is though—big and red," laughed Dom. "We don't know much more about it than that. Not all have seven arms like this one, but they can grow to over three feet in size."

Jake joined in laughing.

"It would be great to collect some samples of the smaller critters to take back with us," Dom said.

Jake powered down the thrusters as Dom took hold of the lever to control the suction sampler. He moved the sampler's funnel close to a bomber worm, applied enough suction force to suck it up into the tube, and then watched it pass through the spring-loaded doors of a collection canister. He lined up the sampler's funnel again, close to a munnopsis, but as he was doing so, *Orion* began to be tossed and jolted around.

"What's causing that?" asked Dom.

"Not sure," said Jake, re-boosting the thrusters. "Seems like the water has become very turbulent."

"Look at your sonar screen, guys," Nick's alarmed voice came over the transmitter. "There's a submarine heading straight for you. Take evasive action immediately."

"Up or down?" asked Jake.

"Up!" Nick replied hastily. "*Orion*'s not quick enough to dive out of its way."

Jake took *Orion* into a sharp rise, holding the controls tightly, his knuckles turning white as he battled to keep her steady in the strong current.

"Let's hope the submarine doesn't do the same when the captain sees us," transmitted Dom.

"I don't think he has seen you," said Nick. "It's not altered its speed or course in any way, and it's virtually upon you."

Suddenly, a deafening clunk jolted and shook *Orion* on the starboard side. Dom and Jake were thrown from their seats. As they picked themselves up, the great looming black mass passed close underneath them.

"Are you OK?" came Nick's concerned voice over the transmitter.

"I think so!" gasped Dom. "What is a submarine doing this far down?"

"Who knows?" replied Nick, sounding relieved. "Must have been one of those titanium-hull nuclear subs on a very secret special operation."

"W-we would have h-had n-no hope if we had collided head on," stuttered Jake. His hands shook as he took hold of the controls.

"That would have caused an international incident," replied Nick. "Is *Orion* damaged?"

Dom maneuvered the video camera around to the starboard side. "There's a scrape or two on the paintwork, but we're not leaking," he reported. "I think we were clipped by the tip of the submarine's fore planes."

"That was close! Are you guys OK to keep going?" asked Nick.

Dom looked at Jake. "How do you feel?"

"Still a little shaken up but if *Orion*'s OK, then so am I."

“I think it’s time to eat our packed lunches,” suggested Dom. “We’ve had an action-packed morning and who knows what else lies ahead?”

A strange-looking octopus with flappy, earlike fins on its head passed the cockpit window.

“Now, *that* was a dumbo octopus!” laughed Dom.

“Weird and wonderful!” exclaimed Jake.

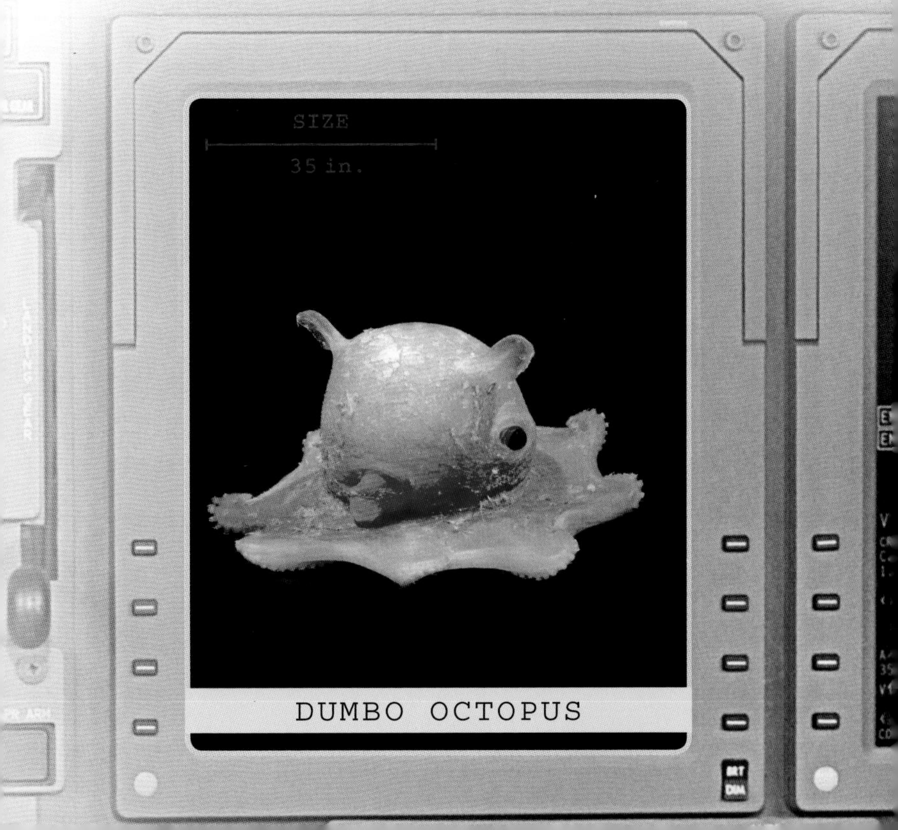

A Nuclear Submarine

While submersibles are designed for short trips, nuclear submarines are able to remain underwater for several months at a time. Most nuclear submarines are used by the military, but a few allow tourists to explore underwater.

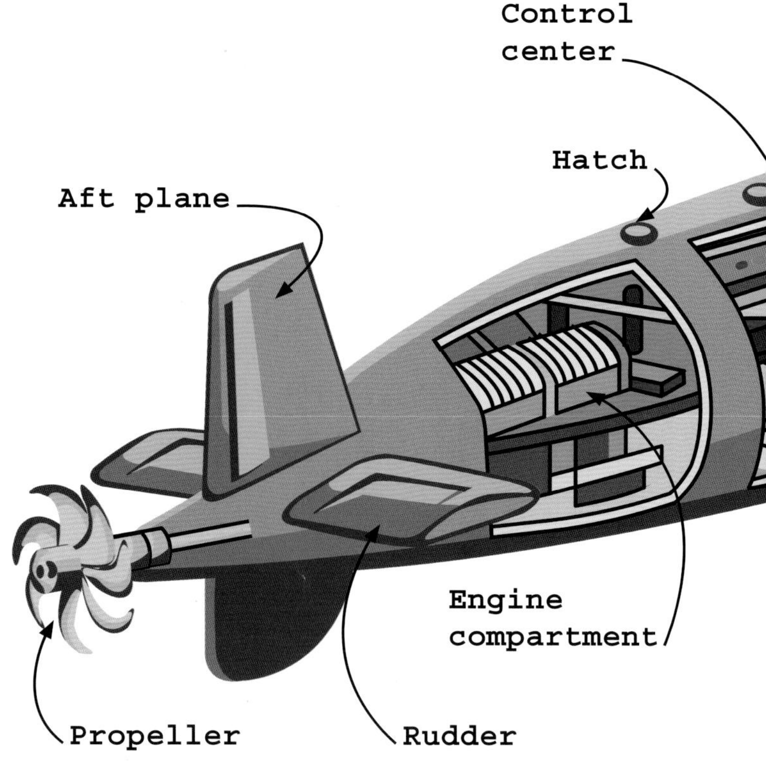

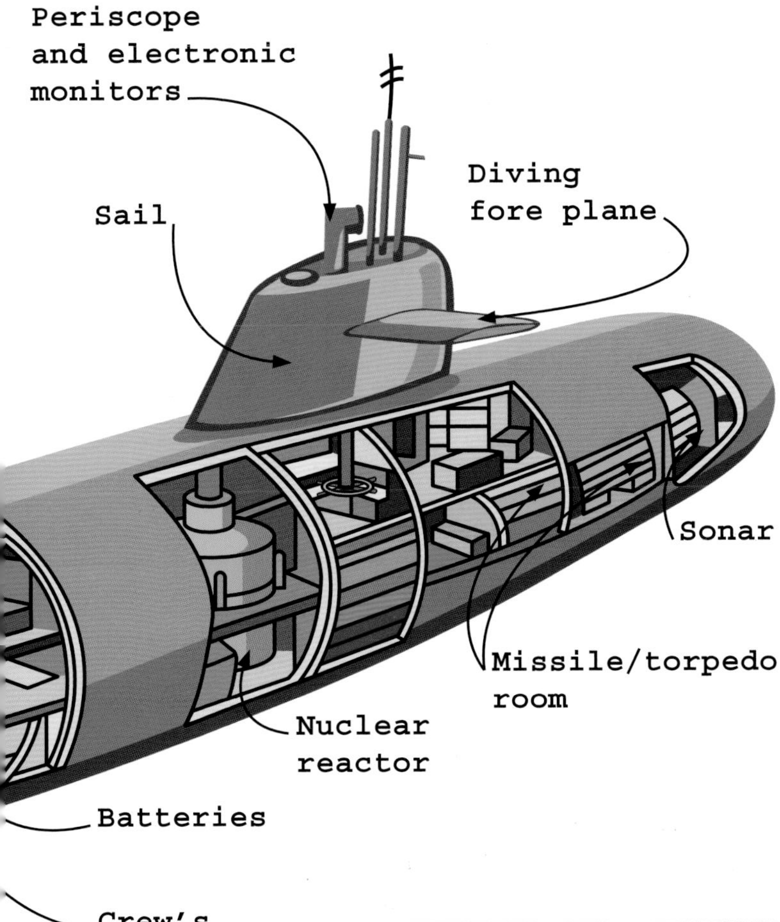

Periscope and electronic monitors

Sail

Diving fore plane

Sonar

Missile/torpedo room

Nuclear reactor

Batteries

Crew's quarters

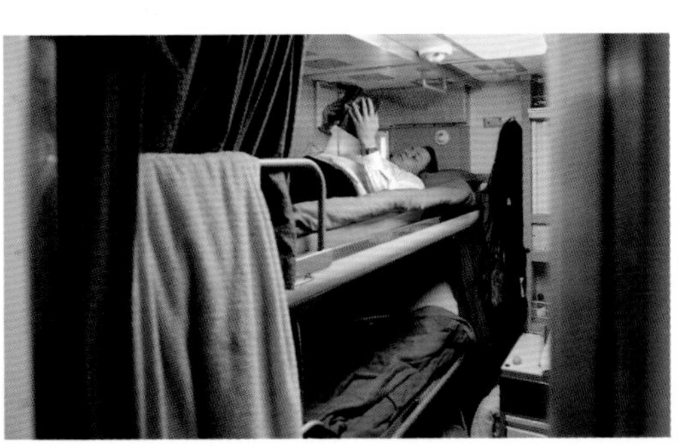

Sleeping quarters for the crew inside a submarine

DATE: 07:07:14 **TIME:** 15:00
TO: Admiral Cavanagh, SSNA
CC: Fleetcaptain Franklin, SSNA
FAX: 00 43 29 87 65 41
FROM: Commander Hudson, *SS Cyclops*
FAX: 00 43 29 41 00 01

TOP SECRET CLASSIFIED

SUBJECT: Investigation report of collision 07:07:14 14:14

For Your Eyes Only, *SS Cyclops* was involved in a collision with an unidentified deep-sea submersible at 14:14 today while on Special Operation: Stealth. Nuclear titanium-hulled *SS Cyclops* sustained minimal damage to the paintwork on her fore planes. The titanium hull and nuclear reactor are fully intact. Two casualties are reported for minor whiplash. Damage sustained to unidentified submersible and the number of their casualties is unknown. Collision was caused due to a sonar screen malfunction. The warning of an approaching unidentified submersible did not appear on the screen.

SS Cyclops was traveling at 40 knots at a depth of 3,280 ft (1,000 m) at UPS location: 11°21'N 142°22'E in the Mariana Trench, Pacific Ocean, when the collision occurred. There was no pre-warning indication of collision on the sonar screen. A head-on collision was only diverted due to action taken by the pilot of the unidentified submersible. The collision caused *SS Cyclops* to shudder slightly. Five crew-members in the control center and sleeping quarters lost their balance. Due to the top-secret nature of Special Ops: Stealth, we did not stop to check the status of the unidentifiable submersible and jeopardize the mission.

After collision, emergency measures were taken. *SS Cyclops* was slowed to 15 knots, and the secondary sonar was used while repairs were being made. Forward sweeps to ensure path ahead is really clear are now being taken every 00:15 minutes. *SS Cyclops* ascended to 1,640 ft (500 m) for 00:30 minutes so that external checks for any damage could be assessed.

As commander of *SS Cyclops*, I believe that no person is to blame for this incident and it was solely due to a technical malfunction. I recommend that sonar systems in nuclear titanium-hulled *SS* submarines should be rigorously checked to work efficiently at this depth.

SS Cyclops will continue Special Ops: Stealth mission through the Mariana Trench and onto the secret location to rendezvous with Stealth agents.

J. Hudson

COMMANDER J. HUDSON
SS Cyclops

Bioluminescent Creatures

In the darkness, some creatures can produce their own light. The glow attracts prey or mates, or helps them to escape.

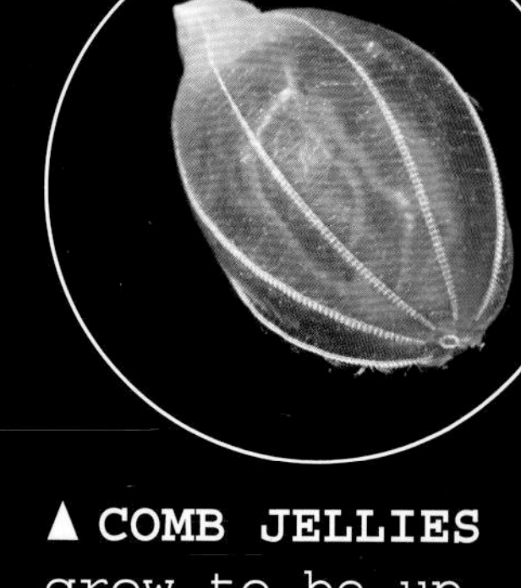

▲ **COMB JELLIES** grow to be up to 6 in. (16 cm) long and use sticky cells on their tentacles to catch prey.

▲ **BIG RED JELLYFISH** can be up to 3 ft (1 m) wide and use between four and seven "arms" to grab food.

► **LANTERNFISH** are less than 6 in. (15 cm) long and produce blue, green, or yellow light.

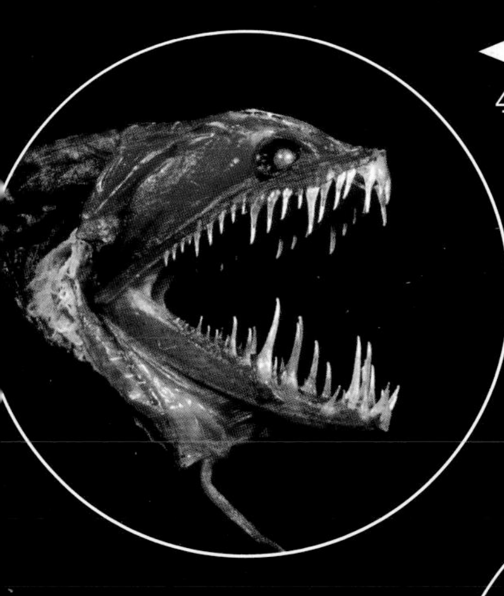

◄ **DRAGONFISH,** from 4–6 in. (10–15 cm) long, use blue or red light to attract prey.

▲ **DUMBO OCTOPUSES,** which can be up to 6 ft (2 m) long, use their earlike fins to move around.

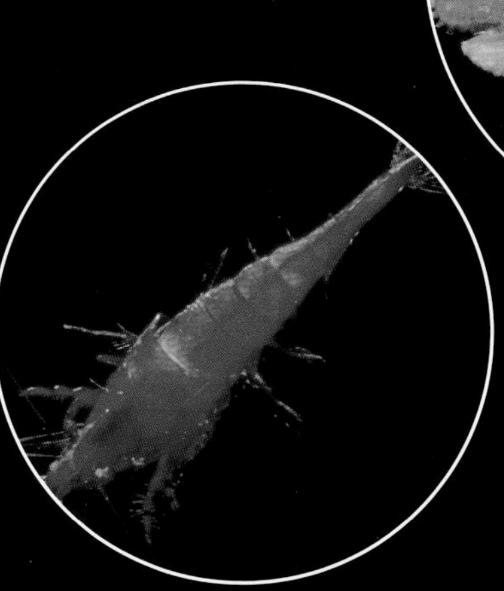

▲ **RED SHRIMP,** about 5 in. (12 cm) long, expel bright blue clouds to confuse predators.

1,000 fathoms
2,000 fathoms
3,000 fathoms
4,000 fathoms
5,000 fathoms

Chapter 3
2,000 - 3,000 Fathoms Deep

Orion continued to descend, leaving behind the luminous creatures. Even these creatures could not exist in the immense water pressure building up.

"The sides of the trench have leveled out. We're on the abyssal plain," said Dom, watching the depth gauge on the computer screen pass 13,000 feet. "Keep your eyes open for gushes of smoke. We want to check out hydrothermal vents before we go much deeper. There should be some around here."

"Something like that?" said Jake, noticing an area of black smoke. He steered *Orion* over to where thick plumes gushed continuously from chimneylike stacks. "That chimney must be at least 16 feet high."

"Look at that odd-shaped one. It looks like a stooped wizard," said Dom, watching fascinated. "That's been formed by all the sulphur and other gases and minerals that are carried up from the Earth in the super-heated water shooting out."

"Sulphur! Thank goodness we're inside *Orion*. Isn't that the gas that smells terrible like rotten eggs? We'd be knocked out!"

"Yes, and from the chemical readings we're receiving from the electrode sensors on the front, there's ammonia and methane gas swirling around in there, too. Quite a cocktail!"

"How on earth are those long wavy tubes and mussels surviving around the stacks?"

"There are bacteria that love the sulphur-based minerals in the water. Look there," Dom said, pointing to some coloring around the vents, "you can see white and orange patches. There are so many bacteria, thriving abundantly, that they've gathered to form mats over the rocks. This is what the tubeworms, shrimp, and many other creatures around here feed on."

"Hey guys, we're receiving great pictures via the video camera," said Nick from the surface. "Can you move in any closer though?"

"Sure," replied Jake, as he maneuvered *Orion* closer toward the vents. The silt on the sea floor whisked up, and a shower of tiny creatures, like snowflakes, spiraled past the window.

"We've disturbed hundreds of tiny crabs," laughed Dom. "Aren't they funny little critters as they just sprawl out and let themselves drift and tumble back down again? Hope you're getting this too, Nick."

"Yes, we're very excited by the pictures."

"Incredible to think that living things can exist here in these extreme conditions," said Dom in awe.

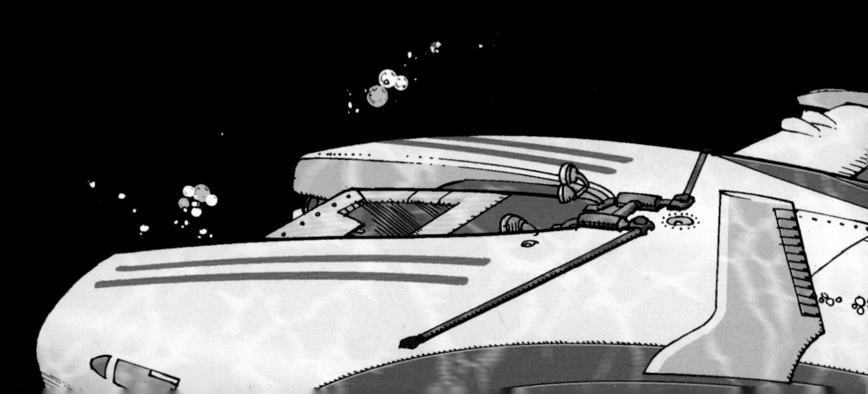

FOCUS ON... Hydrothermal Vents

Hydrothermal vents pepper the mid-ocean ridge, gushing super-heated mineral-rich water into the cold, dark ocean depths. Find out more about these incredible undersea features.

Deep beneath the Pacific Ocean, the sea floor is being ripped apart at the East Pacific rise. This mid-ocean ridge is dotted with volcanic vents and hot springs known as black smokers. The water spewing from the vents is incredibly hot, reaching temperatures of more than 750° F (400° C). Yet vast communities live among the smokers. They get all their energy from the chemicals in the water, instead of from sunlight like nearly all other life on Earth.

The water erupting from the vents is able to reach such extreme temperatures because the high water pressure at this depth stops it from boiling. It is full of dissolved minerals that turn into sooty clouds when the hot vent water makes contact with the near-freezing ocean. Some of the tiny mineral particles that

make the water appear black build up to make tall chimneys around the vents.

At an average depth of about 7,000 ft (2,100 m), a hydrothermal vent seems a challenging place for life to exist. Yet many black smokers are surrounded by clusters of giant tubeworms, huge clams, mussels, and swarms of blind white crabs. They all live on microscopic bacteria that gather chemicals from the vent water, mix them with oxygen to release energy, and use this to make food. The crabs eat the bacteria, but the tubeworms, clams, and mussels grow colonies of bacteria inside their bodies and live on the food they make.

DIVING FOR DISCOVERY

Submersible vehicles used for scientific research into the nature of the oceans explore far deeper than ordinary submarines. Submersibles have played an important part in unlocking the secrets of the sea floor. In 1977, scientists aboard the world's first deep sea submersible *Alvin* discovered the first hydrothermal vent, on the Galapagos Rift off the coast of Ecuador. Scientists had speculated that black smokers might exist, but they had no idea so many strange and unusual sea creatures thrived in the murky depths.

SEA LEVEL
1,000 fathoms
2,000 fathoms
3,000 fathoms
4,000 fathoms
5,000 fathoms
6,000 fathoms

Jake piloted *Orion* around the area of vents. The ocean had come alive with smoking vents, swaying tubeworms, and eels peeking out of cracks in the rocks.

“There’s a bubbling mud vent over there,” Dom exclaimed. “Let’s take a closer look.”

“Is that a flatfish flapping in the mud?” said Jake in surprise.

“It’s a tonguefish,” gasped Dom, “and it’s bathing in 390˚F (200˚C) boiling liquid sulphur.”

“There are more of them on the edge. What are they doing?”

"It looks like they're eating a dead fish that's drifted down from the ocean above," said Dom, peering closely at the camera screen.

"Can you collect a tonguefish and a few rock samples?" requested Nick over the transmitter.

Jake powered down the thrusters to steady *Orion*. Dom used the suction sampler to suck up a tonguefish and then rotated the robotic arm out from under the sub. He then slipped on a glove wired to the controls. Very carefully and slowly, he opened up his fingers. The grabbing end of the robot manipulator mimicked his movements. By watching the video screen, Dom could reach out, turn the manipulator into position, and pick up a loose rock covered with bacteria. Keeping his grip tight, he brought the arm in and dropped the rock into an insulated container.

"That needed a lot of concentration," said Dom, removing the glove, "but it worked really well. It was worth those long hours in the lab to perfect that piece of technology."

"Great skill, Dom," complimented Nick.

Moving on, Jake piloted *Orion* around the protruding vents. Large bubbles were emitting from a few vents.

"Looks like bubbling champagne," remarked Jake.

"They're bubbles of liquid carbon dioxide—a rare sight," replied Dom. "Did you see them too, Nick?"

"Yes, we've noted that along with your location, so we'll be able to report the discovery."

"That vent is getting lively!" exclaimed Jake, pointing at a peaked rock formation gushing out large plumes.

"I think we should avoid getting too close to that one," said Dom.

But just as he finished speaking, the vent erupted, throwing out huge rocks. *Orion* shook violently, caught in the explosion of the gases and heated water. The vast plumes surrounded them, making it impossible for Jake to pilot a getaway. Through the smoke, they could see glowing lava bursting out of the fissure and oozing down the sides. Lava bombs pummeled *Orion*'s shell.

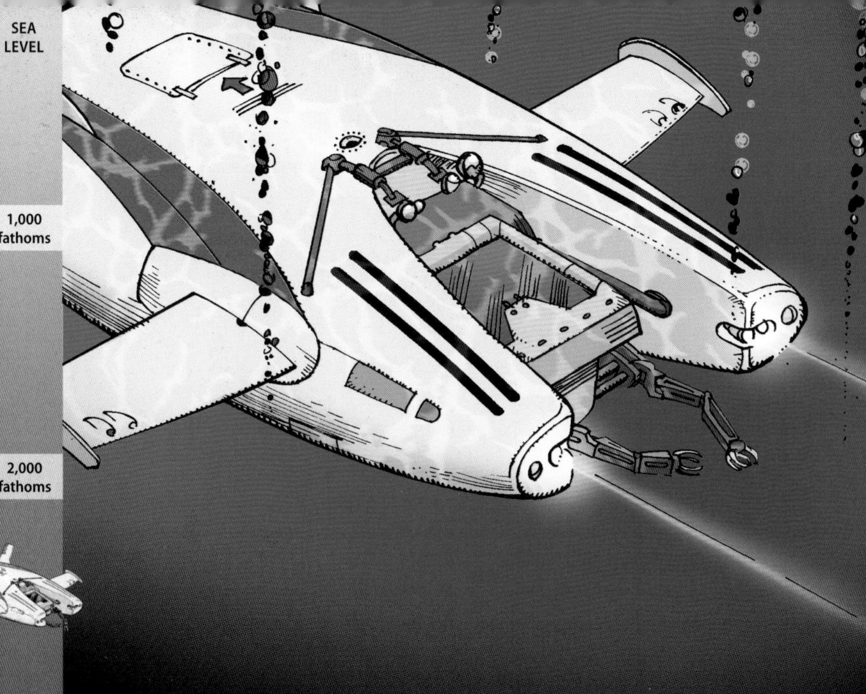

SEA LEVEL

1,000 fathoms

2,000 fathoms

3,000 fathoms

4,000 fathoms

5,000 fathoms

"We have to get out of here, and fast," shouted Dom.

"I can hardly control her." Jake's voice shook with panic. "We're being shaken around too much. Which way should I go? I just can't see. If I go the wrong way

Fortunately, luck was on their side. A gap in the billows of steam revealed a clear space on the port side. As the plume surrounded them again, Jake turned *Orion* to the left and slowly steered her in that direction. A great thud shook *Orion* as yet another lava bomb landed on her hull.

With his pulse racing, Dom leaned forward to glimpse through any openings in the steaming clouds. "Were they about to hit the sides of the trench?" he wondered.

Suddenly, the steam cleared. Ahead, it was clear. In fact, all around them there was just the black ocean of nothingness.

"Excellent steering, Jake," said Nick.

"Where are we?" asked Dom, still disorientated from the shaking. He could feel his pulse slowly returning to a steady pace.

"You've reached the abyss."

The Ocean Bed

The surface of the Earth is divided into large segments called tectonic plates. These plates are always moving and form features such as mountains and valleys. The ocean bed is a part of the land, so it has many similar features.

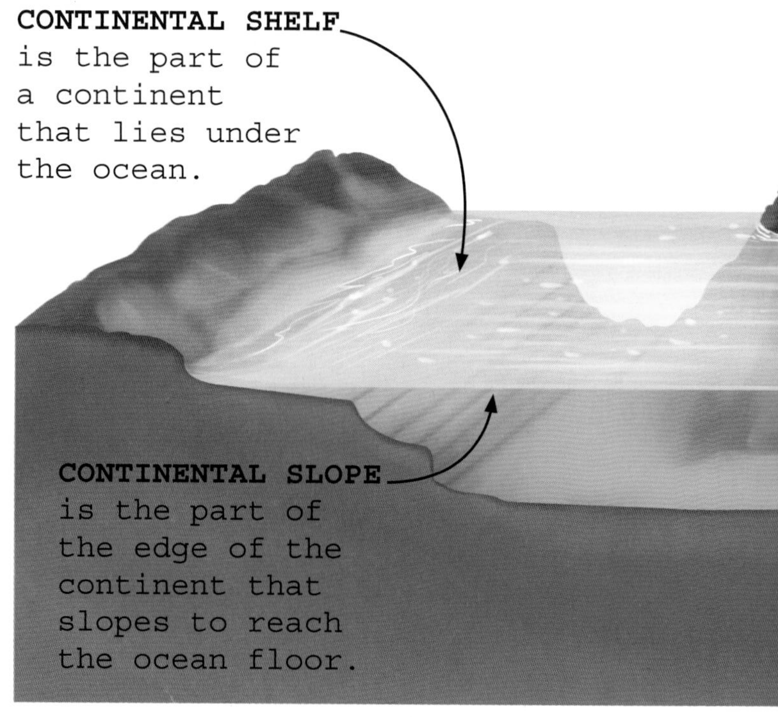

VOLCANIC ISLAND is a landmass formed by the eruption of a volcano in the ocean.

CORAL REEF is an underwater feature that is made up of the hardened remains of sea creatures and is a home for many living sea creatures.

ABYSSAL PLAIN is a flat area of the ocean floor between about 10,000 to 20,000 ft (3,000 and 6,000 m) below the surface.

TRENCH is a long, narrow, and deep dip in the ocean floor.

What is a Hydrothermal Vent?

Hydrothermal vents are small openings in the surface of the Earth that let out heated water. On the ocean floor, these vents are often called black smokers because they release black-colored minerals that look like smoke.

STEP 1.
Tectonic plates separate below the sea floor, forming cracks.

STEP 2.
Seawater seeps into the cracks.

STEP 3.
At the bottom of the crack, hot melted rock near the center of the Earth heats the water.

Tectonic plate movement

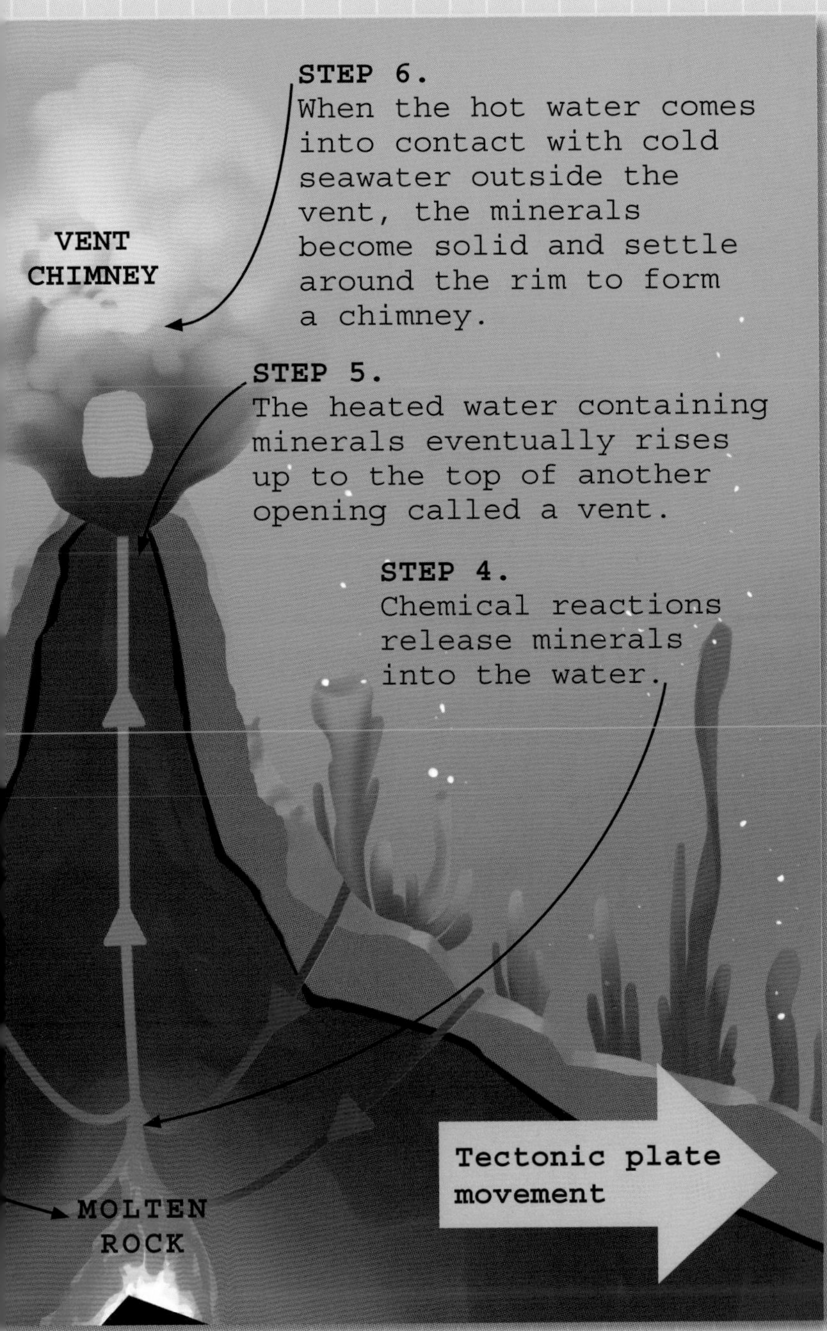

STEP 6.
When the hot water comes into contact with cold seawater outside the vent, the minerals become solid and settle around the rim to form a chimney.

VENT CHIMNEY

STEP 5.
The heated water containing minerals eventually rises up to the top of another opening called a vent.

STEP 4.
Chemical reactions release minerals into the water.

Tectonic plate movement

MOLTEN ROCK

Life Around Vents

Most creatures would be unable to survive around the vents, but some have adapted and thrive in these harsh toxic conditions.

► **Vent crabs,** which can be up to 5 in. (13 cm) long, are red when young but turn white when they grow up.

▲ **Vent shrimp,** 2 in. (5 cm) long, use the bacteria inside them to break down toxic chemicals from the vents.

▲ **Mussels,** about 8 in. (20 cm) long, are usually the first living things to settle near a hydrothermal vent.

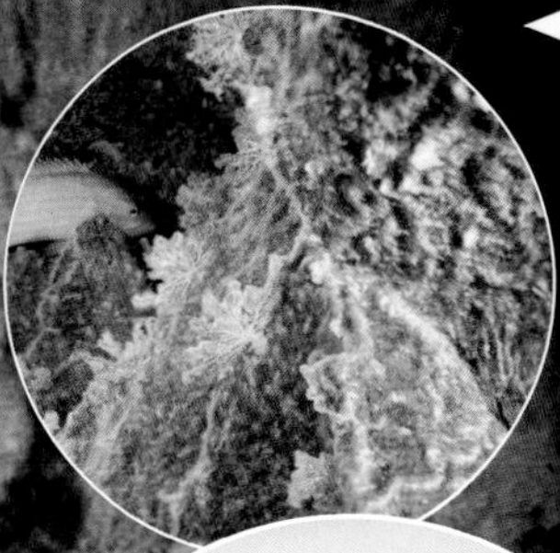

◀ **Microbial mats** are large groups of microscopic living things that work together. The mats can be up to 8 ft (3 m) long.

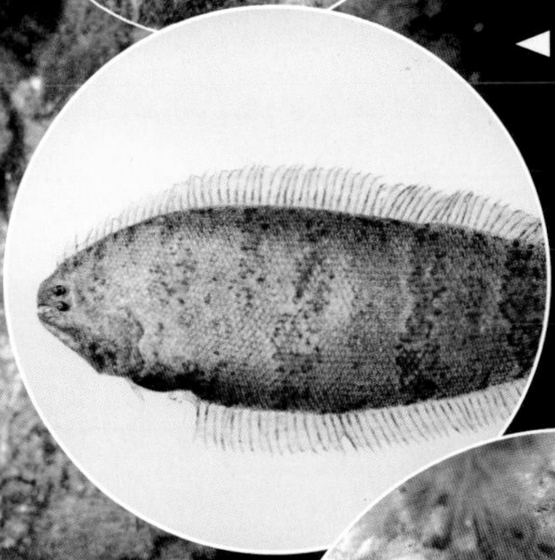

◀ **Tonguefish,** up to 12 in. (30 cm) long, have both eyes on the left sides of their heads.

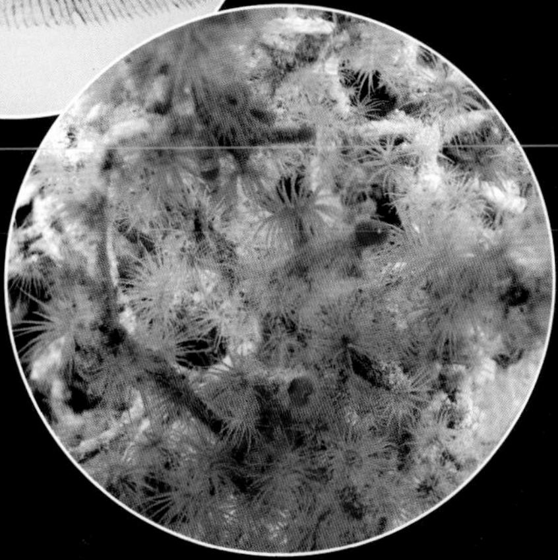

▲ **Tubeworms** can be up to 8 ft (3 m) long and have no mouth, eyes, or stomach. They rely on bacteria that live inside them to break down minerals for food.

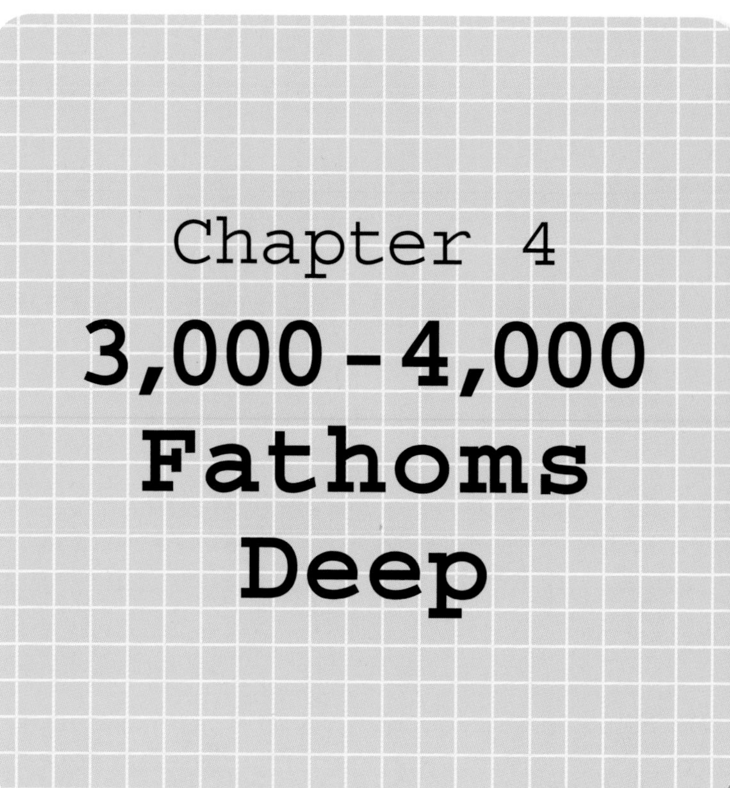

Chapter 4
3,000 - 4,000 Fathoms Deep

"18,000; 18,400; 18,700; 19,000; 19,400. We're now at 19,700 feet," reported Dom into the transmitter as he watched the depth monitor.

The transmission started crackling.

"We won't be in communication with up top for much longer," said Dom, turning to Jake.

Through the crackle, a faint voice from Nick far above could just about be heard. "Line very bad. You're on *(crackle)* your own from now on, guys. Good luck!" Then Nick gasped. "That's weird. There's something *(crackle)* large coming toward you. It's hard to *(crackle)* see. No! It can't be… *(crackle)* Not that big!"

"What is it, Nick?" asked Dom.

"Can't tell but could be a…" The line went dead.

Jake and Dom looked at each other.

"What do you think he was trying to tell us?" Jake asked.

"Not sure, but something big is coming our way," replied Dom. "Nick's right! Look at our sonar screen. Whatever it is, it'll be on top of us soon."

On the screen, a large mass was moving closer steadily. Jake took the joystick controls.

"Which way?"

"Down. Let's get some distance between us and whatever that blob is," suggested Dom.

The numbers started moving on the monitor as Jake maneuvered *Orion* deeper into the dark depths.

"How are we doing?" asked Jake, nervously.

"Not good! It's following us, and it's moving far quicker than us," said Dom. "I estimate it's traveling at three times our speed at least."

"We'll never beat that! Whatever it is, it must be following our lights," said Jake. "Should we turn them off?"

"Not yet. We'll never know how to protect ourselves if we don't know what we're up against. Turn around. Let's face this foe head on," said Dom in a steady voice, although deep inside, his pulse was racing.

Jake turned *Orion* around.

"Over there!" exclaimed Dom, pointing to a large looming shape emerging from out of the inky blackness.

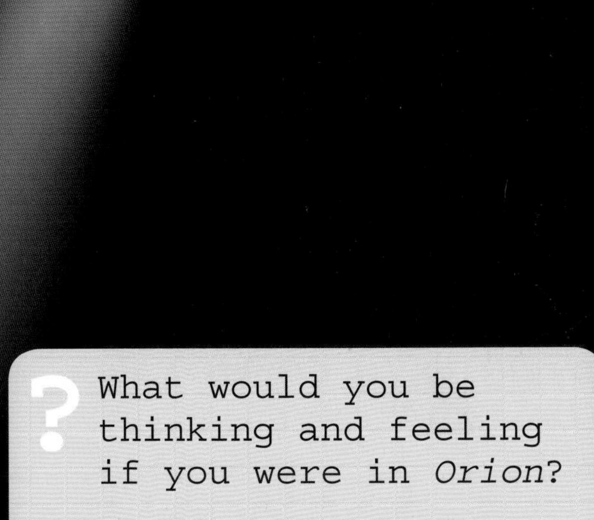

What would you be thinking and feeling if you were in *Orion*?

SEA LEVEL

1,000 fathoms

2,000 fathoms

3,000 fathoms

4,000 fathoms

5,000 fathoms

6,000 fathoms

In the beam of light from *Orion*, Dom and Jake watched as a creature of the deep loomed closer. Eight straggling huge arms stretched outward, squirming like snakes. Two longer tentacles wriggled outward and to the sides rapidly, sweeping the water, searching.

Behind these lethal appendages, a thick, rocket-shaped body appeared, propelled along by a large wavy fin. Enormous eyes that were larger than beach balls were looking directly at Dom and Jake, sitting transfixed inside *Orion*.

"That's not just a giant squid. This one beats the records!" gasped Jake.

"Yes, I estimate that it's at least three times as big as *Orion*," said Dom in awe.

As the giant squid approached, Dom and Jake could see the sharp hooks on some of the suckers more clearly. As the tentacles wriggled, they caught glimpses of the sharp, birdlike beak, opening and closing around the cavernous mouth.

"If we get wrapped up in those tentacles, we'll be crushed completely," said Jake in barely a whisper. He turned his ashen face to Dom. "Any ideas?"

Dom searched his mind for facts about giant squids. Was there something he knew that would help them defend themselves and escape?

Giant Squid Fact File

ESTIMATED LENGTH: 49 ft (15 m)

ESTIMATED SPEED: 23 mph (40 kph)
20 knots

ONLY KNOWN PREDATOR: sperm whale

DEFENSE: squirts a cloud of ink

ATTACK: eight arms with two rows of suckers on lower surface and sharp hooks on some suckers for grabbing and gripping prey.

INTERNAL SHELL called a gladius supports the body. It's made of chitin—a tough, semi-transparent substance that looks like a long piece of plastic.

THREE HEARTS: two for the gills surrounding one larger heart that pumps blood around the body.

INK SAC contains dark, liquid ink, which it squirts out of the funnel when attacked by a predator. The squid hides in the cloud of ink to escape. Scientists think the ink may be luminescent.

BRAIN is the size and shape of a doughnut. Over 80 percent of the brain is given to processing visual information.

Two small bones in the brain called statoliths move around to help the squid know which way up it is in the dark.

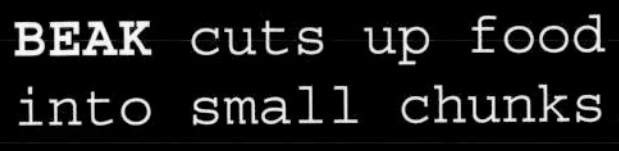

BEAK cuts up food into small chunks.

SUCKERS have sharp hooks.

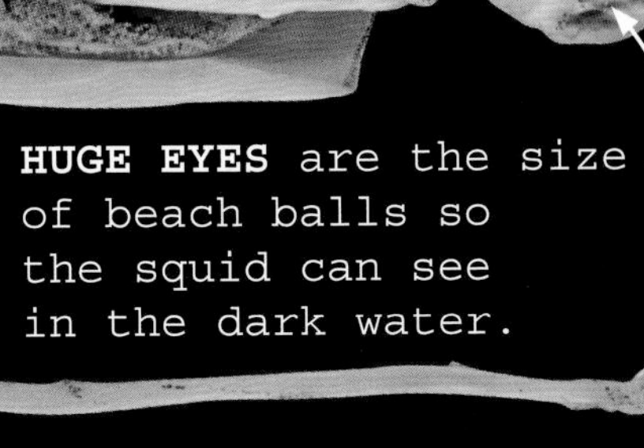

HUGE EYES are the size of beach balls so the squid can see in the dark water.

SEA LEVEL

1,000 fathoms

2,000 fathoms

3,000 fathoms

4,000 fathoms

5,000 fathoms

6,000 fathoms

"I've got an idea!" Dom exclaimed. "We'll try blinding it temporarily with our lights. A squid's greatest sense is vision! This takes up the biggest part of its brain."

"Go on," said Jake.

"Well, if we dazzle it with our lights, we may have a chance of disorienting and confusing it."

But to get the best effect, we'll have to turn them off and sit in darkness ourselves," Jake said worriedly.

"Just for a moment. Then we'll switch them back on. Hopefully, it'll be just like suddenly staring into the glare of the blinding sunlight, and the squid will turn away to avoid."

"It's our best option. The idea will have to work or we'll be crushed. There's no time to delay either. It's nearly caught up to us."

"I'll take the LED switch," instructed Dom. "I'll tell you when I turn them OFF, and then ON. Then be ready to turn the sub and dive deeper."

"OK, I'm ready."

Dom watched the gigantic squid swim closer and closer, its tentacles splaying out in front.

"Just a little closer," Dom whispered under his breath. "Steady now..." Then he shouted, "Lights OFF!"

He flicked the switch, and they were plunged into a black darkness—darker than any moonless night. Keeping his fingers on the control stick, Jake listened, waiting for Dom's next vital instruction. He could hear his own heart thumping, the whir of the engine, and Dom's quickened breathing.

"ON!" Dom said as he flicked the switch again.

A sudden bright blinding glare of brilliant light shone out into the dark ocean, filling the cockpit, too. Jake and Dom were forced to close their eyes, but concentrating on the feel of the controls, Jake took *Orion* into a dive and turned away from the squid.

As their eyes became accustomed to the glare once again, they looked out above and behind to spy the squid. Had their plan worked, or were they seconds away from being grabbed?

? Close your eyes. What's the closest sound you can hear?

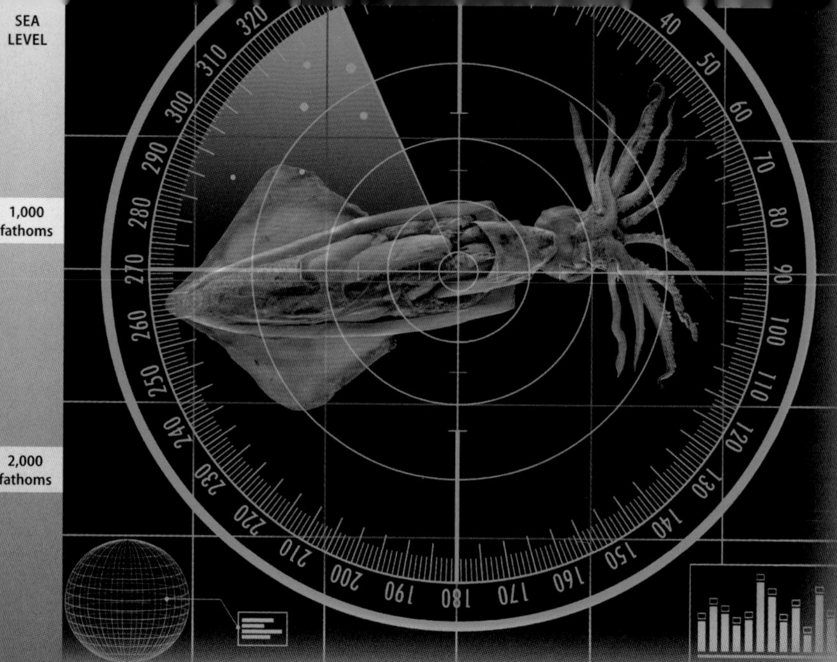

Dom looked down at the sonar screen.

"It worked!" he gasped with relief. "Look! It's turned and fled." The screen showed the large mass moving swiftly away in the opposite direction.

"Thank goodness," sighed Jake, pulling forward the control stick to bring the sub into a gentler dive. "That was a bit too close for comfort."

"*Orion*'s designed to withstand the crushing water pressure down here, but I wouldn't have wanted to test her strength against that beast's bite!" said Dom.

"How strong is *Orion?*"

"At the bottom, she'll have to contend with water pressure that's as strong as if three Range Rovers were resting on your toe. She'll be fine though. This metallic shell has been tested under greater pressure and she only shrank about three inches."

"That's good to know. We shouldn't notice the difference then."

"That's right!" Dom confirmed. "Are you OK at the controls? I'd like to write a report about that encounter before we see any other creatures down here."

"Sure," said Jake. "That squid was easily one for the record books. The guys up top will definitely be excited about this discovery."

Dom started his account, as many other intrepid divers had done before.

The Hunt for the Kraken

Since ancient times, sailors told of enormous monsters with tentacles, such as the Kraken. Scientists now think that these were sightings of the giant squid and the colossal squid, but these giants of the deep remain a mystery.

1555

Although legends of a sea monster with tentacles had existed since the 13th century, Olaus Magnus was the first person to call the monster a Kraken.

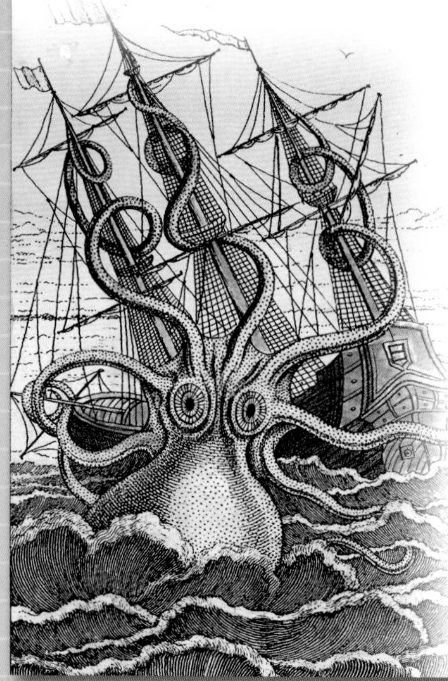

1755

Erik Pontoppidan published a description of a sea serpent seen from a ship off the coast of Norway in 1746. He called it the Kraken.

1857

Japetus Steenstrup identified the giant squid as a unique species after he saw a beak collected from a dead squid that had washed ashore.

1925

Two enormous tentacles were found in the stomach of a sperm whale. These tentacles were identified as being from a squid even larger than the giant squid—the colossal squid.

2001

Scientists led by Steve O'Shea caught the first living giant squid off the coast of New Zealand. They caught seven baby squids that died shortly after.

2003

The first complete colossal squid specimen was caught, with a body of about 8 ft (2.5 m). Only about half a dozen colossal squid have ever been found.

2005

Tsunemi Kubodera and Kyoichi Mori presented the first underwater photographs of a live giant squid in its natural habitat.

2007

The largest-known specimen of colossal squid was caught off the coast of Antarctica (above). It was almost 33 ft (10 m) long and was put on display in the Te Papa museum in New Zealand.

2012

An expedition led by Tsunemi Kubodera off Japan's Ogasawara Islands captured the first video footage of the giant squid in its natural habitat.

Chapter 5
4,000 - 6,000 Fathoms Deep

Jake watched the UPS digits on the computer screen, recording their position. 11°21'N 142°12'E. "We're right above Challenger Deep," he announced, "the deepest part of all the oceans. The only way now is straight down."

"It's time for some dinner and a quick nap then," said Dom, as he stood up to shake and stretch his legs.

He had to bend over slightly, but *Orion*'s cockpit was roomier than most manned submersibles.

Jake switched on the automatic pilot control. The thrusters twisted to propel *Orion* downward. From now until she reached the bottom, *Orion* would steadily drop. Dom dimmed the LED lights. The ocean was eerily dark, still, and lifeless.

"How long do you estimate it'll take?"

"We're just over halfway with 16,400 feet still to drop. I'll slow her down so we can have a couple of hours' rest," said Jake. He bit into his sub sandwich. Until this moment, everything had been so action packed that he hadn't realized how hungry he actually was. Dom, beside him, had already closed his eyes, taking advantage of this quiet time. Jake wondered what they would find at the bottom. Would there be nothing, or would they make some new discovery?

Sonar Mapping of the Mariana Trench

Sonar mapping uses sound to detect objects and depths underwater. Sound is played into the water, and when the sound reaches an object or the ocean floor, it bounces back. The time it takes for the sound to return indicates the shape and distance of an object.

Challenger Deep
35,814 ft (10,916 m) down

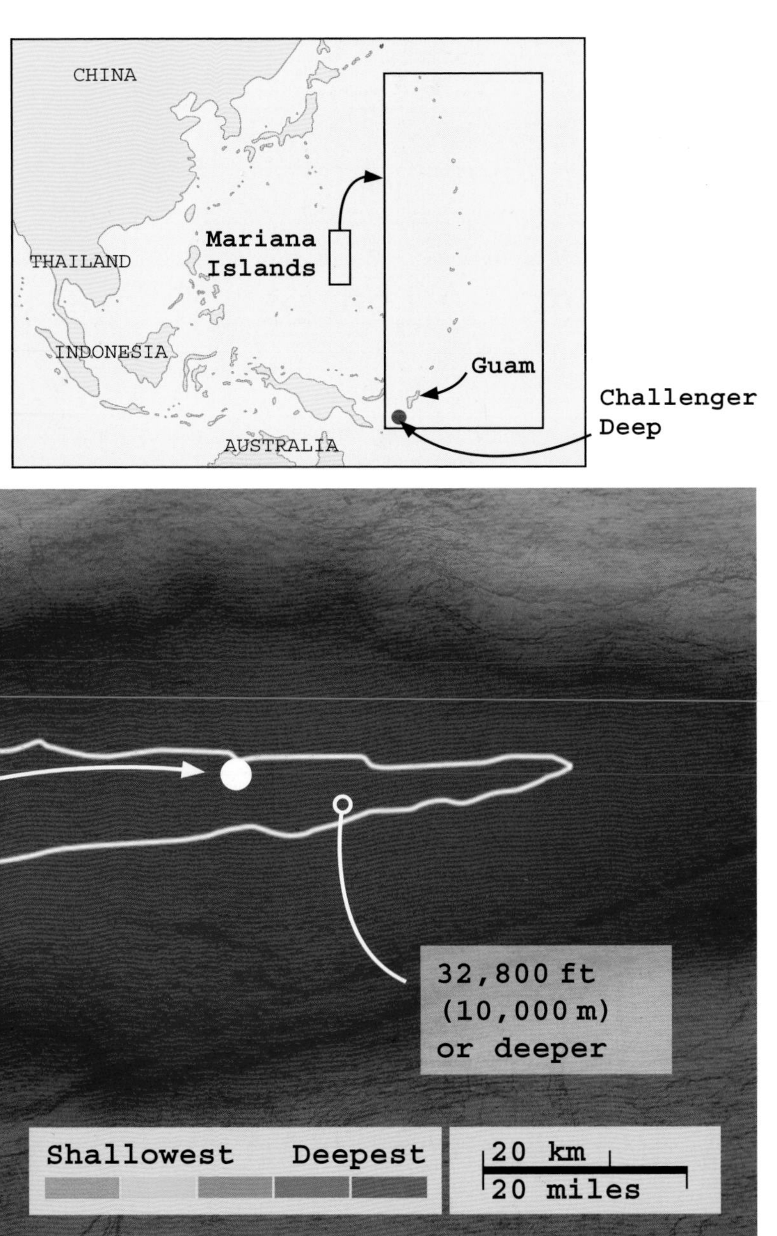
CHINA
THAILAND
INDONESIA
AUSTRALIA
Mariana Islands
Guam
Challenger Deep
32,800 ft (10,000 m) or deeper
Shallowest
Deepest
20 km
20 miles

The beep, beep of the control's alarm woke Jake and Dom from their brief snooze. They had arrived. The alarm signaled that they were just 164 feet from the ocean floor. They were deeper than Mount Everest, the tallest mountain, is tall. They were closer to the center of the Earth than any person in the world. They were in a place where only a handful of other people had ever reached.

Dom peered out of the cockpit window as Jake switched the controls back into manual mode.

1,000 fathoms

2,000 fathoms

3,000 fathoms

4,000 fathoms

5,000 fathoms

6,000 fathoms

"Can you see anything?" asked Jake.

"Not at the moment," replied Dom, looking out into the blackness. He raised the magnifying camera and turned it on. The screen showed nothing—no life at all.

Dom turned the lights to full beam. "Let's see what it looks like out there."

As their eyes became accustomed to the brightness, they began to make out an eerie, lunarlike landscape. The ocean floor was barren and colorless with silky sand and the odd rocky boulder. Nothing moved.

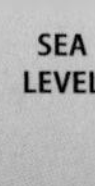

SIZE
2 in.
XENOPHYOPHORE

"Let's drop the bait and see if anything comes to bite it," said Dom. He released the spring door to a container underneath *Orion*. A foot-long piece of fish meat dropped onto the ocean floor. They sat watching the bait intently.

After a while of nothing happening, Dom said, "We had better start collecting rock and sediment samples at least." He tried not to convey his disappointment as he slipped on the electronic glove and guided the robot manipulator into position.

Opening the grabber by moving his fingers, it reached to pick up a rock. As the grabber disturbed the surrounding sediment, something caught Dom's eye. A small, spongelike, ball-shaped creature was inching its way slowly across, leaving a trail of slime.

"It's a xenophyophore. Can you see any others? They're often bigger," said Dom excitedly.

Jake peered out as he very slowly steered *Orion* over the trench's floor. "What are they?"

"They are large, single-celled critters that fan out or curl up into discs or frilly, spongelike shapes. There are a couple over there!" Dom and Jake peered down at the strange creatures.

"We can see them because silt and even their own poop stick to their outer parts," Dom continued. "They go around sifting and eating the sediment, feeding on the minerals it contains from the Earth's metals and dead animals. Microbes too small to see are probably feeding on them."

After Dom took a sample, Jake maneuvered *Orion* back to the bait. As they approached, they could see movement—a swarm of tiny creatures. Looking at the camera screen, they could make out hundreds of flealike creatures.

"These are amphipods, but they are larger than most," Dom explained. "I wondered if we would see them down here, since they've been spotted before at these depths."

"They are nothing new then?"

"I'm afraid not. Both these species have been recorded before."

Just then, three large pink fish swam into the scene.

"Are these a new species?" asked Jake, as he watched them swishing around the bait. Some more joined them.

"They look like snailfish, and a family of them, too," said Dom. "But," he continued excitedly, "they may be a new species. We won't know until we get one back to the lab."

"Why are they not eating the bait?"

"They're after the micro-shrimp that feed on the rotting fish remains."

"Something has just wriggled past the screen," observed Jake.

Dom moved the camera around, scanning the ocean and trying to track the creature. “I know you’re there. Come and show yourself. Found you! It’s a bristly seaworm.”

They watched the seaworm ripple its bristles to propel itself along. Suddenly there was a swish, and the worm was swallowed up. The camera was staring into a swollen snout and a toothy grin.

Jake jumped with surprise, “Now, he’s ugly!”

As the creature swerved past the lights, they caught a glimpse of a translucent, eellike creature about six inches long.

“Its side angle is no better. You can see through to its bones,” said Jake.

“You can’t help what you look like down here. You’re only designed for survival, and anyway, it doesn’t matter—nothing can see you anyway,” laughed Dom.

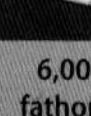

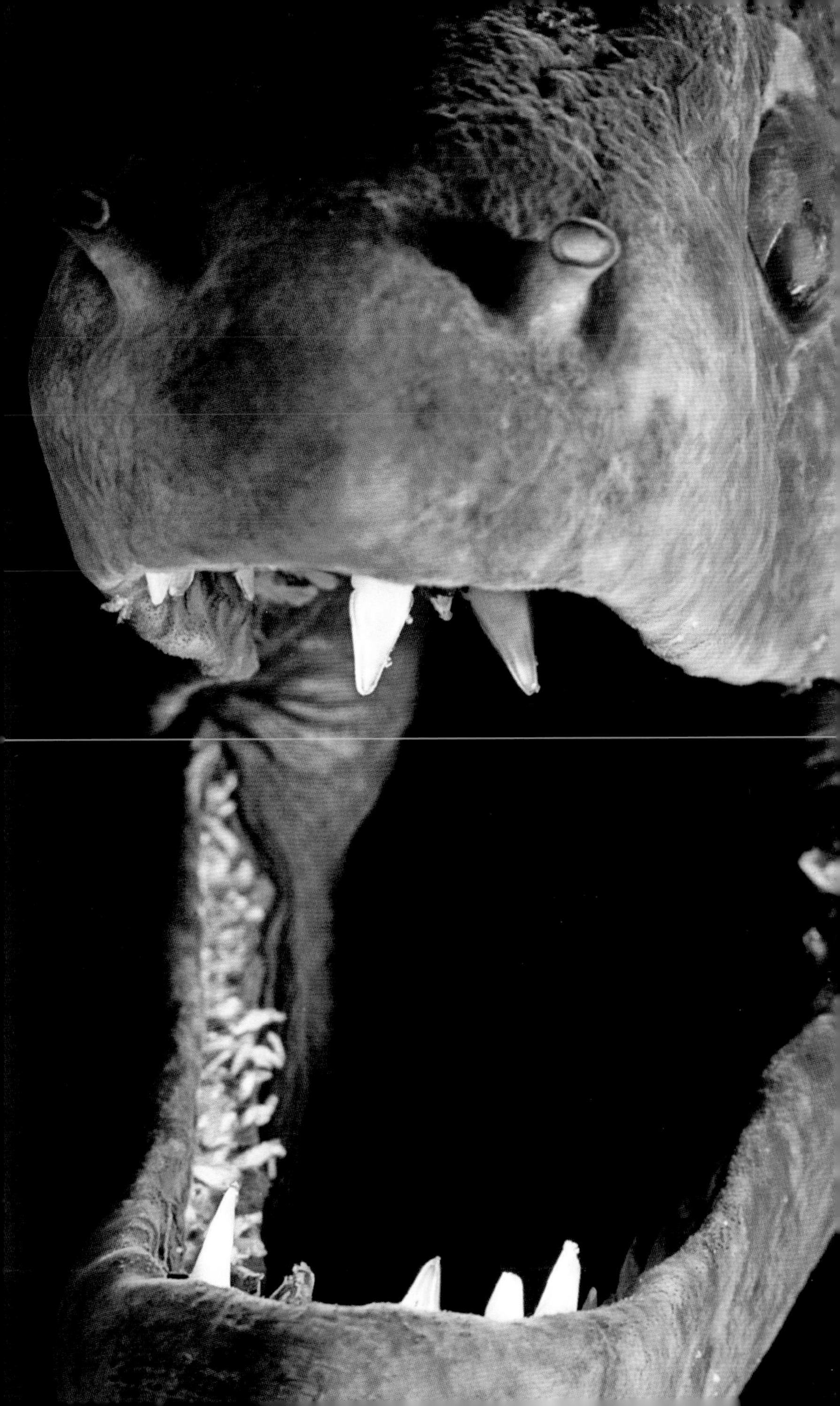

"We need to get going soon," said Jake, "or else we'll run out of oxygen before we get back to the surface."

"Just a little longer to collect some sediment samples," said Dom, putting on the glove to control the robot arm again.

Jake positioned *Orion* once more above the ocean floor and lowered the power to the thrusters. Dom controlled the grabber to pick up the scoop attachment and then extended the arm into the sediment. As the scoop went through the sediment, it jammed on something hard. Dom tried to pull the scoop away but the arm resisted.

"I can't believe it! The scoop is stuck," said Dom, annoyed.

"Give it a jiggle," suggested Jake.

"I'm trying, but it's not budging."

"We need to get going. I'm sure we have enough samples. Just leave the scoop down here. It can be our mark for future visitors to find."

Dom tried to let go of the scoop, but his fingers were unable to open. "The grabber, too, is stuck in there." Beads of sweat began to build up on his forehead and trickle down his face.

? Time is running out. What do you think Dom and Jake should do?

Seabed Survival

In the total blackness and extreme pressures of the deep seabed, the creatures have adapted special ways to survive and find food that has drifted down from above.

► **XENOPHYOPHORES,** which are more than 4 in. (10 cm) long, live by wrapping their "arms", or pseudopods, around small particles of decaying food and "swallowing" them into their bodies.

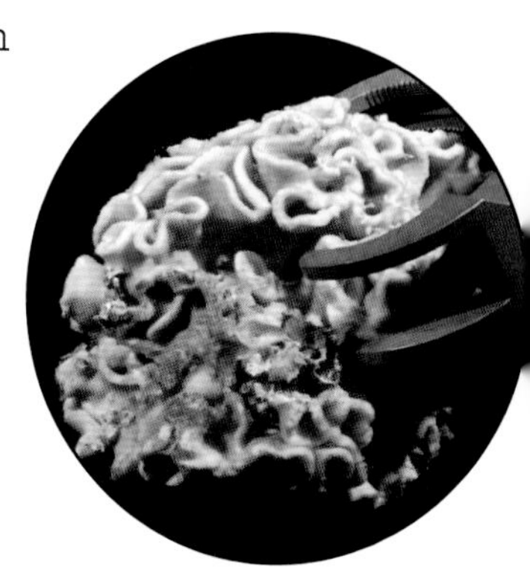

◄ **POLYCHAETES** are worms that grow up to 5 in. (13 cm) long and are protected in these harsh conditions by bacteria that live on their backs.

► **RATTAILS,** usually 4 in.–5 ft (10 cm–1.5 m) long, use their strong sense of smell to find food in the dark.

◄ **CUSK EELS,** up to 6.5 in. (16.5 cm) long, sense vibrations with their snouts in order to find food and get around in the dark.

◄ **FLEALIKE AMPHIPODS,** about 11 in. (28 cm) long, feed on sunken pieces of sea plants.

► **SNAILFISH,** 12 in. (30 cm) long, use vibration sensors on their snouts to find their way and food in the total darkness.

The History of Submersibles

Most submersibles are made up of a sphere-shaped metal chamber encased in a hull.

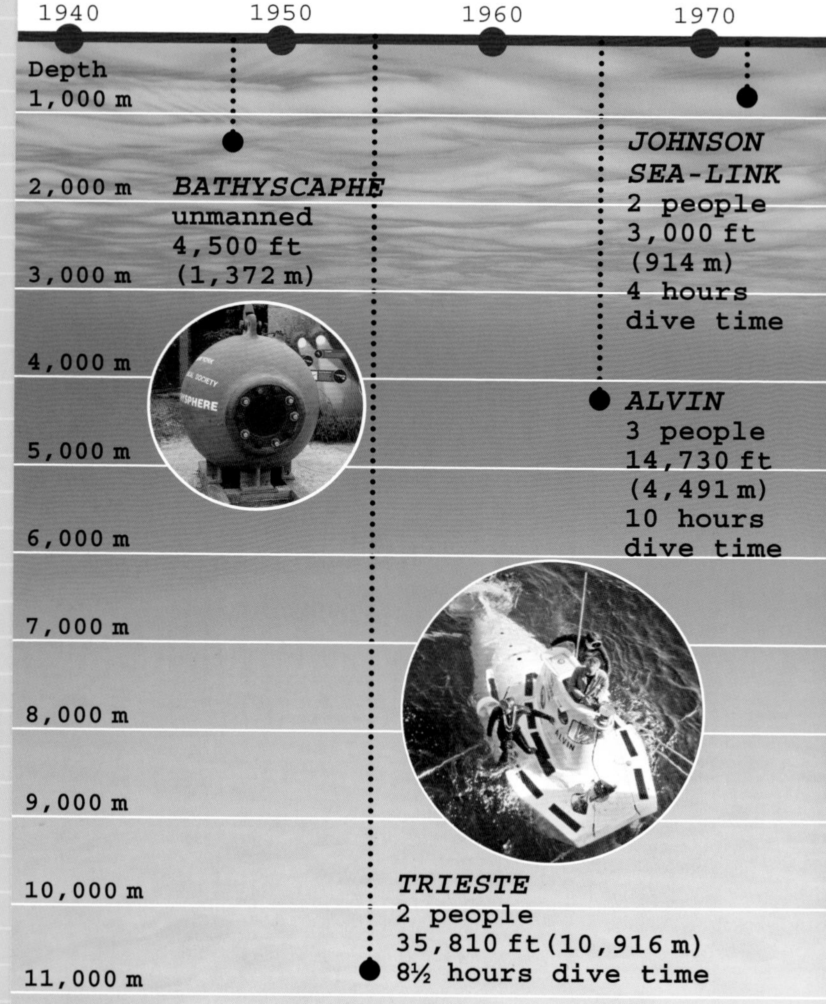

The sphere shape is chosen because it can withstand the great pressure deep underwater better than other shapes. Submersibles also contain air tanks or foam to aid flotation and heavy weights (ballast) that are dropped when the vehicle rises to the surface.

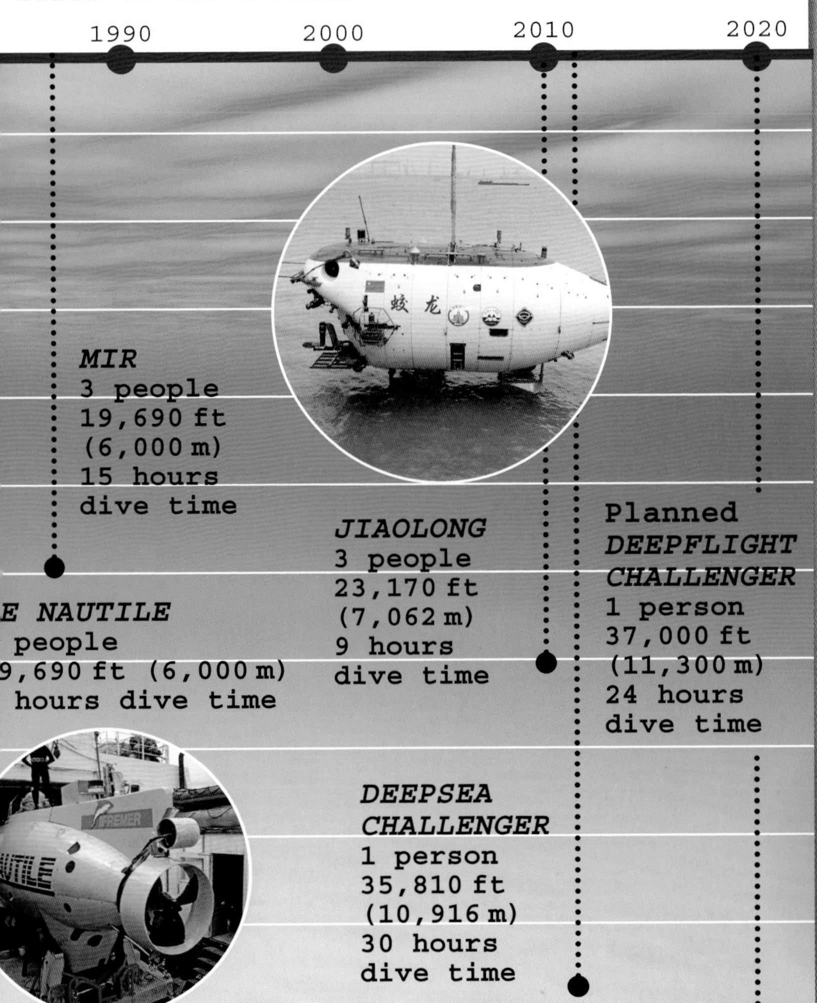

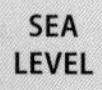

Chapter 6
The Ascent

"Take off the glove. Perhaps we can pry them open together," suggested Jake.

Dom twisted off the glove, and then he and Jake pulled at the fingers of the glove to open them up, but with no luck. They struggled for a while, persevering.

"The arm is completely stuck," Dom said, finally giving up.

"We need to head back. We won't have enough oxygen if we hang around any longer," Jake said, worried.

"But how do we pull away? The robot arm is fixed to *Orion*."

"We can only hope that *Orion* is stronger, and as the thrusters pull upward, the arm rips off."

Jake rotated the thrusters to move upward and increased the power. As *Orion* lifted, the arm contorted but continued to resist the pull.

"It looks like I'll need full power to break it off. Hold on. It could be a rocky lift off," said Jake with determination.

Dom watched as the arm strained, taking on the weight of *Orion*, but finally the metal snapped. Suddenly released, *Orion* jerked upward. Left behind on the ocean floor was the lower limb of the arm, wires flapping, protruding like a piece of a sunken shipwreck.

Jake steadied *Orion* and gradually the ascent began. The distance between them and the ocean floor increased foot by foot. They didn't need to worry about getting the bends or any other illness related to the change in water pressure. The cockpit had remained at one pressure throughout the trip.

"I'll keep the video camera on," said Dom, "just in case we see anything of interest. Although it's pitch black in the ocean outside, you never know what strange creatures might pass by."

"We'll be unable to stop to take a good look though," said Jake, anxiously. "The delay when loosening the robot arm used up valuable time on our oxygen supply. We've only enough now for a couple more hours."

"That should be plenty," reassured Dom. "At the rate we're ascending, we only need just over an hour's supply. *Orion* is rising perfectly."

He passed an apple from the food supplies to Jake and took another for himself. "Breakfast, kind of," he thought.

They had both completely lost track of time while being in such a timeless, oceanic world. In the darkness, day and night means nothing to the creatures of this habitat.

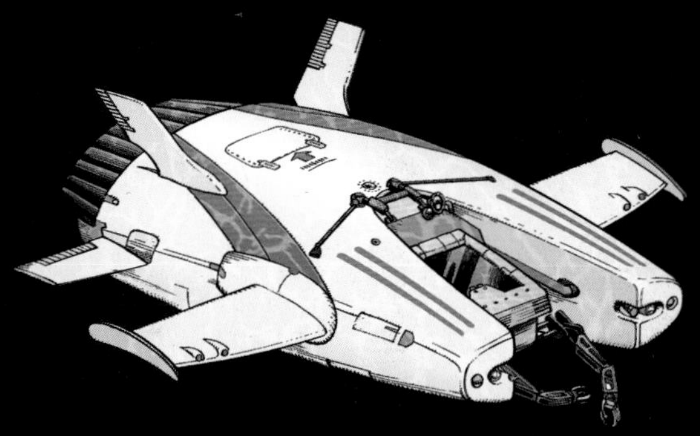

Dom was brought out of his ponderings by a beep on the sonar screen. A flashing red, streamlined shape was heading their way. It was just over 12 miles away, but moving swiftly.

"Do you have any idea what that might be?" asked Jake.

"Not really, but at that size I don't think we want to find out," replied Dom. "Let's keep space between us and head directly for the surface."

Jake kept *Orion* on course with full power from the thrusters. Dom continued to monitor the screen. He didn't want to alarm Jake, but the creature was traveling much faster than they were moving. Also, as it moved closer, the sonar could more accurately show the creature's shape and size. The red shape had turned into an outline of a shark. But this was no ordinary great white. This one was almost 100 feet long.

“That’s prehistoric size,” murmured Dom to himself. Could the reports that a megalodon lurked in these waters be true? They hadn’t died out millions of years ago with the dinosaurs?

As *Orion* rose through the water, so too did this giant shark. “It’s definitely following us,” thought Dom. “*Orion* must have something on its hull that the creature has picked up the scent from.”

"How much further, Jake?" asked Dom, trying not to sound concerned.

"There's another 13,000 feet," informed Jake. "We should be able to receive transmissions from Nick on *Andromeda* by now."

"I'll give it a shot," said Dom, turning on the transmitter. "Hello Nick, are you there?"

"Yes, good to hear from you again," replied Nick. "Your signal is loud and clear. Did you make it all the way down?"

" Yes, I'll start sending back the video recordings."

" You can wait until you're back to the surface to sort out that."

"I'm not sure if we're going to make it. Have you seen the sonar screen? We have a huge shark following us very swiftly. It seems pretty determined to make us its lunch."

"How long do you think it'll be before you see it?"

"Ten minutes or so, I think," estimated Dom. "We have no way of defending ourselves against that 30,000-pound crushing bite."

"We can only hope that it won't come to that," responded Nick, trying to be encouraging and light-hearted. "I'll start receiving recordings, but only because we're eager to see them."

"Do we really have no chance?" said Jake, worried.

"Sharks are supreme hunters, and if I'm right, this one chasing us is the fiercest of them all," explained Dom honestly. "Either it'll attack us from behind, taking a huge bite first and then returning to finish us off like a great white hunts, or it'll disable us by sheering off *Orion*'s side wings before lunging in for a final kill. That's how paleontologists think the megalodon hunted."

"Those options don't sound good."

"We can only hope that it'll want to do some investigation first, just take a small nip, and then realize *Orion* doesn't taste that good and will leave us alone." Dom looked down at the sonar screen. "Not long to find out now. See! The sonar shows it's nearly upon us and sneaking up from below."

"Nick, if we don't survive this," continued Dom into the transmitter, "hope you can salvage the *Orion* and the data she holds about our journey. She's been incredible."

"You have been, too!" exclaimed Nick. "It's coming in from behind now. Brace yourselves."

? How would you describe the attack and finish the story?

Megalodon Fact File

LIVED: 16–1.6 million years ago

ESTIMATED LENGTH: 53 ft (16 m)

ESTIMATED WEIGHT: 60,000 lbs (27,000 kg)

HUNTING TACTICS: rushed at prey from beneath; used teeth and strong jaws to disable it by biting off the fins

CLOSEST LIVING RELATIVE: great white shark

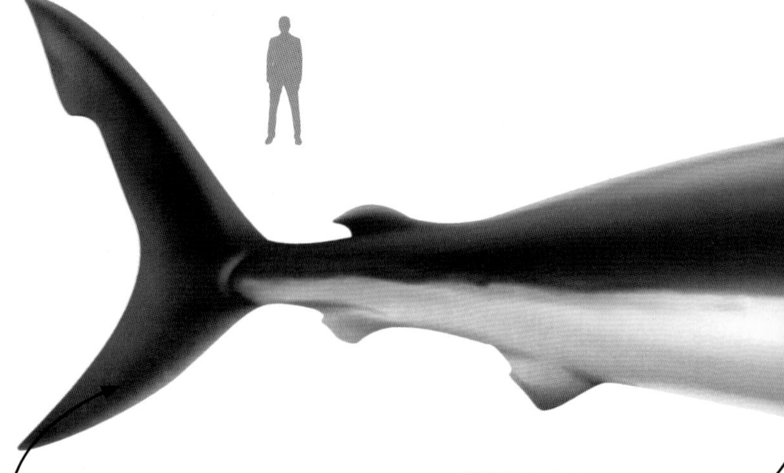

TAIL FIN moved from side to side to allow the megalodon to move forward through water.

SKELETON made of cartilage instead of bone and provided greater flexibility, allowing the megalodon to move quickly through water.

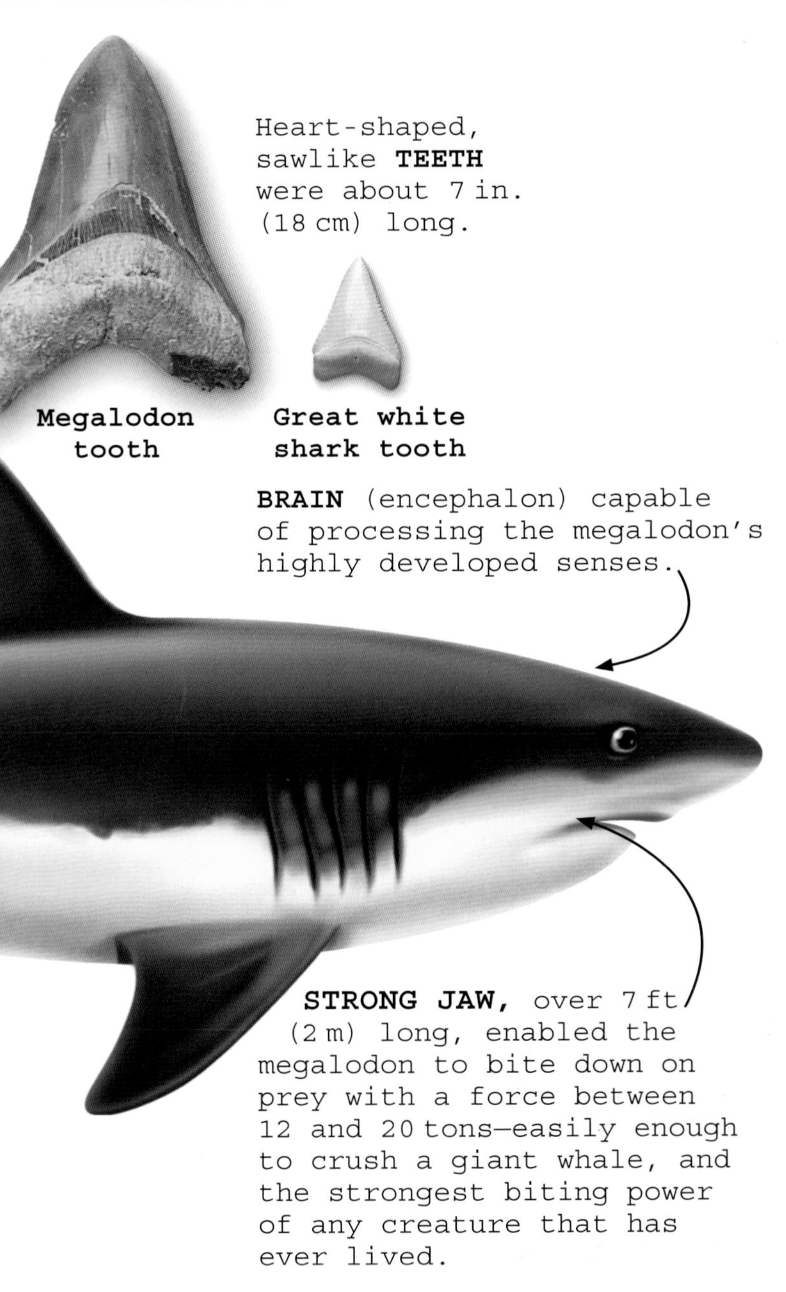
Heart-shaped, sawlike **TEETH** were about 7 in. (18 cm) long.
Megalodon tooth
Great white shark tooth
BRAIN (encephalon) capable of processing the megalodon's highly developed senses.
STRONG JAW, over 7 ft (2 m) long, enabled the megalodon to bite down on prey with a force between 12 and 20 tons—easily enough to crush a giant whale, and the strongest biting power of any creature that has ever lived.

Chapter 7
The Adventure Ends

Thump! The megalodon hit *Orion*'s right side with an incredible force of strength, sending *Orion* spiraling downward out of control.

Jake and Dom gripped their seats as they watched the huge muscular body of the megalodon pass by the window. Would it decide to return for a bite? They were transfixed as the gigantic shark turned with great agility to face them, staring straight into their eyes. It seemed confused at having hit a hard object, but its pain turned to anger. It advanced, grinning and closing in foot by foot. As it approached, it opened its mouth wide, revealing rows of long, serrated, heart-shaped teeth.

Suddenly the beast swerved and, missing *Orion* by a few feet, propelled itself upward like a torpedo. Following its movement, Jake and Dom watched as it attacked a 60-foot-long whale above them.

"Where did that whale come from?" asked Jake in shock.

"Who knows? But that sperm whale has just saved our lives," responded Dom. "Let's get out of here, while the megalodon's busy."

Jake took the controls again and piloted *Orion* once more toward the surface. Out of the window on the starboard side, Dom watched as the megalodon lunged in for a final fatal bite of the helpless sperm whale.

Sperm Whale Fact File

ESTIMATED LENGTH: 49–59 ft (15–18 m)

ESTIMATED WEIGHT: 70,000–88,000 lbs (31,750–40,800 kg)

AVERAGE SPEED: 23 mph (37 kph)

PREY: squid

NOTCHED TAIL FLIPPERS (flukes) measuring 16 ft (5 m) from top to tip allow whales to move quickly through water.

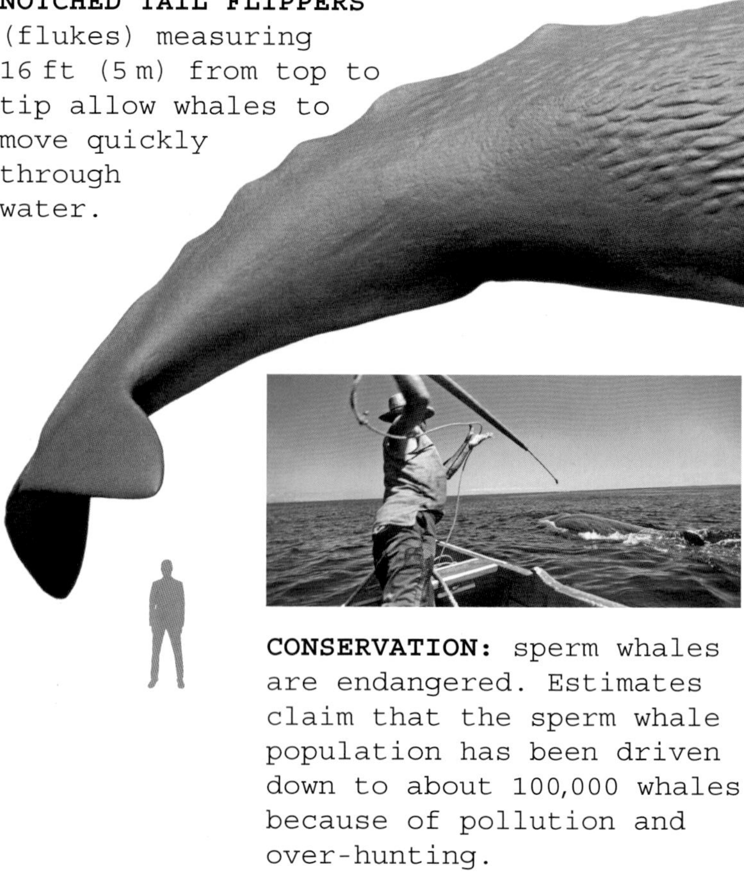

CONSERVATION: sperm whales are endangered. Estimates claim that the sperm whale population has been driven down to about 100,000 whales because of pollution and over-hunting.

LARGE, BLOCK-SHAPED HEAD makes up about a third of the whale's body length and more than a third of its weight.

ASYMMETRICAL SKULL helps whales to hear under water.

BLOWHOLE

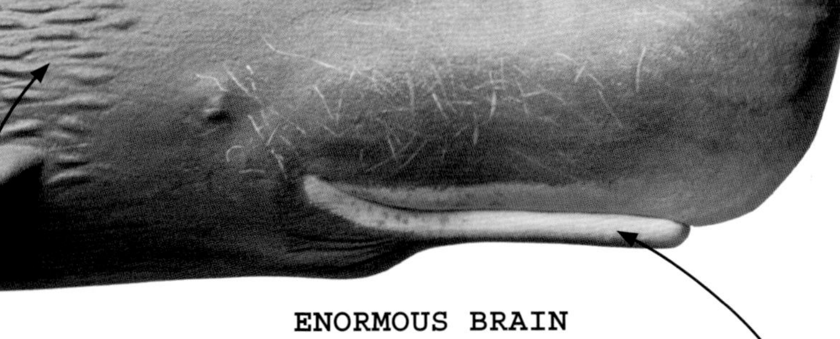

WRINKLY SKIN is unique to the sperm whale.

ENORMOUS BRAIN weighs about 9 lbs (4 kg). It is the largest of any animal that has ever lived.

LOWER JAW contains 18 to 25 cone-shaped teeth, which help when eating squid. Each tooth can weigh 7 lb (3 kg) and be 8 in. (20 cm) long.

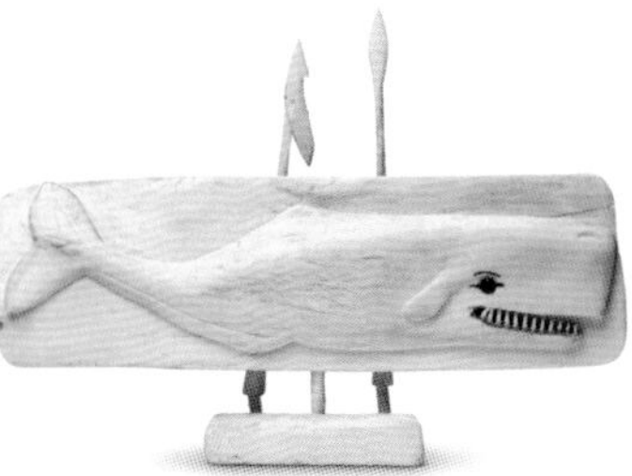

Carved whale bone

"That was a narrow escape," gasped Nick over the transmitter, "but great to see you're coming home."

"We're not out of danger yet," replied Jake. He noticed that the red warning light of the oxygen supply indicator had just come on. "We're dangerously close to running out of oxygen, and we've still got another 6,000 feet to climb."

"Hang in there, guys," replied Nick. "We'll make sure everything is swift and smooth for your retrieval once you reach the surface."

"Thanks, we'll need that," said Dom. "We're passing through the midnight zone full of those bioluminescent creatures once again." He dimmed the LED lights and raised the magnifying camera. Jake and Dom watched together as the microscopic creatures drifted and danced, lit up like magical fairy lights. *Orion* glided through a bloom of ghostly jellyfish with silvery sparkling tentacles.

Look back at pages 40–41. Which is your favorite bioluminescent creature?

“The world is a very different place down here,” remarked Dom, “and there’s still so much to discover about the lives of these mysterious creatures.”

A glint of sunlight caught the hull of *Orion* as she glided out of the darkness into the warm blue waters. The submersible was surrounded by an abundance of sea life. Flashes of silvers, blues, and yellows shimmered in the sun’s rays as fish darted past. A group of Pacific reef sharks swam proudly, sweeping their tails from side to side.

However, inside *Orion’s* cockpit, the conditions had deteriorated.

The final puffs of oxygen had been extracted from the system. Jake and Dom were feeling faint in the stale air.

"How are you guys doing?" asked Nick, greatly concerned.

"Not good at all," replied Dom faintly. It took all his effort to respond as he sat limp in his seat.

"I'm switching to autopilot," gasped Jake. His hands flicked the switch and then dropped weakly into his lap.

"That was an amazing adventure," sighed Dom as he closed his eyes.

It was now left to *Orion* to bring them up the last 650 feet to the surface.

Orion broke through the surface of the water with hardly a splash.

Jess, looking out from the deck of *Andromeda*, spotted the hull glinting in the midday sun. "Over there!" she cried, pointing out to the gliding craft.

The support boat sped out, and Raoul leapt across, attaching the towrope. As he quickly opened the hatch, the cockpit was filled with a gush of fresh air and warmth. He slipped through the opening and wriggled through into the cockpit.

Jake and Dom sat slumped in their seats. Raoul powered down the thrusters and then turned to take their pulses. Dom's was faint but steady, while he could hardly find Jake's at all.

He wriggled out of the hatch. The support boat had already brought *Orion* almost alongside *Andromeda*.

"They're both looking bad, especially Jake," he shouted up to Karl. One at a time, Karl threw down two oxygen

masks with a reservoir bag attached. Raoul slipped back into the cockpit and placed the masks onto Jake and Dom.

He then attached the crane cables, and signaled to Ben at the crane's controls. Slowly, *Orion* was lifted out of the water and across to the deck of the ship and lowered to rest back in her cradle.

Epilogue

A few hours later, Jake and Dom stood beside *Orion* examining her scrapes and bumps with Nick and the rest of *Andromeda*'s crew.

"That gash was where the nuclear submarine's fore planes swiped us," pointed out Jake. "That jolt threw us from our seats."

Dom brushed his hand across a huge dent, "This must be where she received the force of the megalodon's attack."

He bent down to examine the remaining part of the robotic manipulator arm. "We left a part of her down on the ocean floor."

"It was worth it," said Nick. "We've already started testing the samples of the rocks and creatures in the containers. The snailfish does appear to be a new species, so who's it going to be named after? Will it be Dom or Jake?"

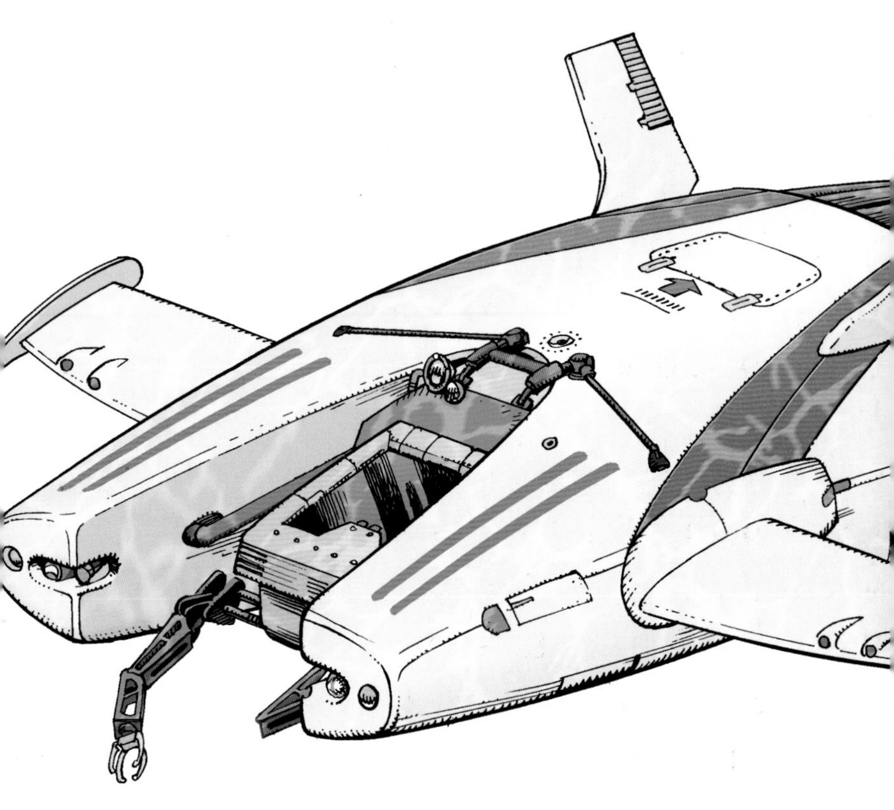

"*Orion*," said Dom and Jake together without hesitation. "She's the one who took us down, brought us safely back from the bottom of the ocean, and protected us from the terrors we encountered. Three cheers for *Orion*!"

The Daily Journal

EXPLORERS REACH DEEPEST POINT IN THE OCEAN AND ENCOUNTER MYTHICAL BEAST

By Ray Bass
Science Reporter, Mariana Islands

Explorers Jake Sturgeon and Dom Marlin have returned to the surface after diving nearly 7 miles (11 km) down to the deepest part of the ocean, the Challenger Deep in the Pacific Ocean, and coming face-to-face with the prehistoric megalodon along the way.

They made the descent in a submersible called *Orion*, on a 24-hour action-packed mission, spending more than 3 hours exploring the ocean floor.

"Everything just goes pitch black for hours—that's when things start creeping up on you," Dr. Marlin, an oceanographer, told *The Daily Journal*.

Marlin and Sturgeon, the pilot of *Orion*, are two of only a handful of people to have visited the ocean's deepest depths.

Marlin has spent the past few years working with a team of engineers to design and build *Orion*.

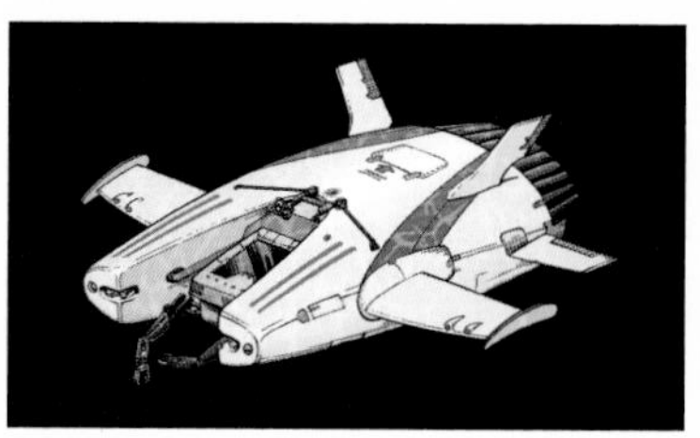

The submersible *Orion*

Sturgeon describes it as an "airplane" that glides through the water, allowing it to move around easily near the ocean floor.

The sub is equipped with LED lights, underwater cameras, and a robotic arm to help collect samples.

The excitement felt by Marlin at being faced with such a terrific

A megalodon, thought to have died out 1.6 million years ago.

opportunity drove away any fears he had.

"It really was a once-in-a-lifetime opportunity to study deep-sea life up close. I knew it would provide answers to many questions and give rise to new ones," he said.

Sturgeon was less relaxed about the expedition.

"A lot can go wrong when you're that deep in the ocean. It was definitely risky."

The explorers say that the primary purpose of the mission was scientific research.

"We were hoping to discover some new species, and I think we have," said Marlin.

Among the samples they collected, they discovered a new species of snailfish near the ocean floor.

But the journey didn't always run smoothly.

"We had several near misses: we narrowly avoided a collision with a nuclear submarine and came across a colossal squid at least three times the size of *Orion*," Sturgeon said.

"We were even attacked by a giant shark! We think it might have been a prehistoric megalodon. We were saved when a sperm whale diverted the shark's attention."

The megalodon is thought to have died out 1.6 million years ago. If they are right, it will be a major scientific discovery.

The deep sea is helping scientists study how species live in its hostile conditions, how earthquakes and volcanic eruptions occur, and how the Earth's climate is changing.

Marlin hopes this will mark the beginning of an age of deep-sea exploration.

"For decades, everyone thought space was the final frontier, but we know more about space than we do about the depths of the ocean—and this is right on our own home planet!"

CHALLENGING THE DEEP: an interview with *Orion*'s crew

Oceanographer Dom Marlin and submersible pilot Jake Sturgeon have just returned from the deepest point in the ocean, the Challenger Deep. They are two of only a few people to have been there. Reporter Marina Crabbe had a chance to talk to them.

MARINA: What's it like down there?

DOM: It's dark and quiet. The ocean floor looks like the surface of the moon—all rocks and sand. The creatures down there really look weird!

MARINA: What did you find most surprising?

JAKE: I knew we would see some unusual sea life, but one thing I didn't expect was coming face-to-face with a nuclear submarine!

MARINA: Why are you so interested in the deep sea?

DOM: The ocean's depths are the most mysterious part of the Earth, so it's really thrilling to discover what's out there. But there's also a lot we can learn from life and the atmosphere deep under water.

JAKE: And I'm always up for an adventure!

MARINA: Jake, how did you become a submersible pilot? Is there a training course for that?

JAKE: Actually, there is! It teaches you everything you need to know. I started out as an airline pilot, though, and it's surprising how similar airplanes and submersibles can be sometimes.

MARINA: What were your main goals before setting out on this expedition? Did you achieve them?

DOM: We wanted to explore life around the hydrothermal volcanic vents and in the Challenger Deep by photographing and taking samples of what we found there. I would say we achieved all of our goals, and even made an unexpected discovery.

MARINA: Which was?

DOM: That the prehistoric megalodon—a giant shark long thought to have been extinct—may still be alive deep in the Pacific Ocean.

MARINA: How did you feel when you first set off on the expedition?

JAKE: Nervous! I've piloted plenty of submersibles, but there's always a risk. Plus, I'd never been that deep down, where there's no possibility of rescue.

DOM: I couldn't wait to get down there. I was eager to see things that I'd only heard about and didn't even have a chance to think about what might go wrong.

MARINA: Tell me about the submersible, *Orion*. What makes it so special?

DOM: *Orion* is fully equipped with video cameras, a robot manipulator, and scientific measurement tools. Unlike other submersibles, though, it has wings that enable it to glide through water like an airplane.

MARINA: What's next for you?

DOM: This is just the tip of the iceberg. Some other teams are sending unmanned submersibles down, which can spend a lot longer down there. It would be great to get involved in that. I'm hoping another dive is on the cards for us. Are you up for it, Jake?

JAKE: Well, Dom, give me a couple of months to recover, and then you won't be able to keep me away!

Ocean Exploration Quiz

See if you can remember the answers to these questions about what you have read.

1. What was the name of *Orion*'s support ship on the surface?
2. What do zooplankton eat?
3. What was Dom hoping to see when they got to the abyssal plain?
4. What are coral reefs made of?
5. Why are hydrothermal vents on the ocean floor sometimes called "black smokers"?
6. What are usually the first living beings to settle near a hydrothermal vent?

7. What is the giant squid's only known predator?
8. How did *Orion* manage to escape from the colossal squid?

9. What is the deepest part of the ocean called?

10. How do snailfish find food in the darkness of the deep seabed?

11. What did Jake and Dom leave behind on the ocean floor?

12. What was the name of the first submersible to make it to 35,810 ft below the surface of the ocean?

13. How long ago did the megalodon live?

14. What saved Jake and Dom's lives when the megalodon attacked them?

15. How much does a sperm whale's brain weigh?

Answers on page 125.

Glossary

CONTINENT

A large land mass.

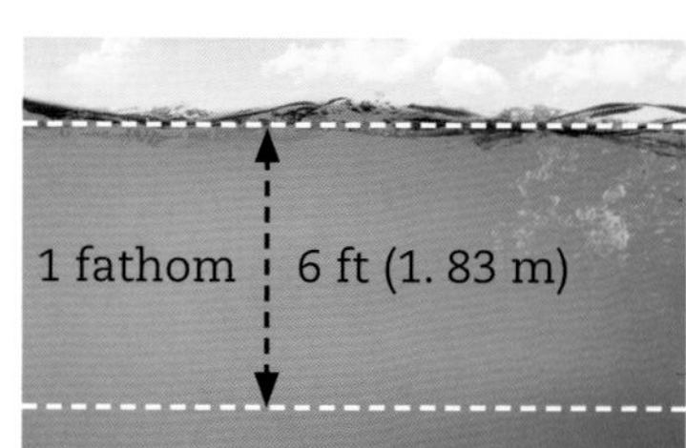

FATHOM

A unit of marine depths equal to 6 ft (1.83 m).

FLOTATION

The process of floating.

GLOBAL POSITIONING SYSTEM (GPS)

A satellite system that records an exact location. UPS is used underwater.

HYDRAULIC

Moved or operated by a liquid, such as water, under pressure.

HYDROPHONE

An electronic instrument that detects and locates sounds under water.

HYDROTHERMAL

Hot water that has been heated from under the Earth's surface.

LIGHT EMITTING DIODE (LED)

An electronic device that changes voltage into light.

MICROBES

A microscopic living thing such as a type of bacteria or virus.

PLANKTON

A collection of microscopic animals and plants that drift in the ocean.

PORT

The left-hand side of a ship or aircraft if looking forward.

SEAMOUNT

A large underwater mountain that has a peak under the ocean's surface.

STARBOARD

The right-hand side of a ship or aircraft if looking forward.

TECTONIC PLATES

Blocks of the Earth's crust that move constantly, pushing or pulling away from each other.

TENTACLE

An extended, flexible body part around the mouth of a squid, used for feeling, grasping, and moving.

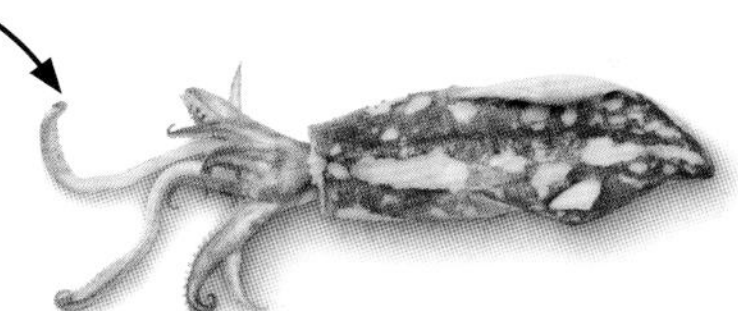

TURBULENT

Rough and agitated.

Answers to the Ocean Exploration Quiz:

1. *Andromeda*; **2.** Phytoplankton; **3.** Hydrothermal vents; **4.** Hardened remains of sea creatures; **5.** They expel black-colored minerals that look like smoke; **6.** Mussels; **7.** Sperm whale; **8.** It stunned the squid with its LED light, and the squid swam away; **9.** The Challenger Deep; **10.** They have vibration sensors that help them to detect food; **11.** *Orion*'s robot arm; **12.** *Trieste*; **13.** 16–1.6 million years ago; **14.** A sperm whale; **15.** About 9 lb (4 kg).

About the Author

Deborah Lock is Senior Editor at Dorling Kindersley as well as a writer and mother of two. She was previously a teacher and has worked at Dorling Kindersley since 1998, producing children's nonfiction books about all kinds of topics, from history, science, and politics to art, music, gardening, pirates, and mythical beasts. She is the series editor of the DK Readers reading program and is currently working on some innovative new products for the best-selling educational Made Easy workbooks program. She spends her leisure time involved with youth work and has a passion for singing, drama, and dancing.

About the Consultant

Dr. Linda Gambrell, Distinguished Professor of Education at Clemson University, has served as President of the National Reading Conference, the College Reading Association, and the International Reading Association. She is also reading consultant to the *DK Readers*.

Here are some other DK Adventures you might enjoy.

Horse Club
Emma is so excited—she is going to horseback-riding camp with her older sister!

***Star Wars*: Jedi Battles**
Join the Jedi on their epic adventures and exciting battles. Meet brave Jedi Knights who fight for justice across the galaxy.

***Star Wars*: Sith Wars**
Meet the Sith Lords who are trying to take over the galaxy. Discover their evil plans and deadly armies.

Index